THE SPORTS M(

The Sports M

How To Go Further Faster and Achieve Your Sporting Dream

by Lee Ness

Published by Lee Ness

Createspace Edition

Author's Website

leeness.co.uk

Other books by this Author

FICTION

HOPLITE - PART 1: LYSANDER (Olympian Book 1)

HOPLITE – PART 2: THE GENERAL (Olympian Book 1)

HOPLITE – PART 3: TRAINING (Olympian Book 1)

D.E.M. - DEUS EX MACHINA

This book is dedicated to my wife Mandy, who has supported me in coaching, writing and life plus my two boys, Jake and Ethan, who have made me into a coach.

It is also dedicated to the athletes I have coached and my fellow coaches, from all sports past and present. I have learned far more from you than you have from me.

Foreword

The challenge isn't someone else.

The Challenge is within
It's the aching in your lungs
And the burning in your legs,
And the voice inside you that yells 'CAN'T'.
But you don't listen,
You just push harder.
Then you hear a voice whisper 'can',
And you realise the person you thought you were
Is no match for the one you really are.

Author Unknown

Introduction

Introduction

My name is Lee Ness and I am an Athletics Coach. That is not my day job, but if I wanted to describe myself that is how I would like to do it. I have been a coach for 10 years, coaching football, cycling and athletics. I have managed people in my day job for 20 years. I have used these experiences to study which people do well and which don't at all levels and, more importantly, why that is the case.

I believe that talent is not given and that no-one is born with it; talent is earned and anyone can earn it if they have the desire. This book has been written for athletes who want to earn their talent to become the best at what they do and the coaches and parents of those athletes.

This is a culmination of many hours of reading and researching sports books and articles, as well as biographies and autobiographies of the sporting greats in a wide range of sports; from Michael Johnson to Michael Jordan, and many in-between. My experience also comes from observing and talking to people both in business and in sport. I have searched for the threads that run through each story, bringing them together as a single resource to help you become the best in your sport.

I have not written this looking from a top down perspective as, when you are at the top, it is easy to forget what you did to get there, who your first coaches were, and what you did on a day-to-day basis. A cynic might say that when you are at the top it may suit you to embellish some elements and leave others out. It might be of use to make it seem easier than it was, or harder than it was. It might just be that it was a long road and it is not easy to remember such things clearly.

Reading this book will start you off on a long, hard road that will help you reach the top of your sport. It is about the grit and the grind of starting out as an athlete. It is about how your life is affected by your journey and how you have to adapt to be successful. Being successful in sport is not about where you come from. Having a privileged background or a poor one is irrelevant; for every sporting great from one background there will be one from the opposite end of the spectrum and everything in between.

I have not included the occasional seemingly accidental sports star for whom everything just fell into place and who just happened to be in the right place at the right time. Everyone would like to be plucked from obscurity and thrust into international greatness because that would be easy, but in reality life is just not like that and, in my research, I just haven't found anyone that it has happened to.

This book is about making the opportunities happen yourself, rather than waiting for them and hoping they will. It is about preparing yourself and putting yourself in the right place. It is about dealing with adversity, overcoming all the obstacles and defeating the odds – because the odds **are** against you. You can overcome the odds, but it is a long road and the sooner you start and the harder you work, the sooner you can get to where you

want to be.
If you would like a taste of what this book is about, there are two short videos you should watch, which are completely unrelated to the book, but sum it up quite nicely. The videos feature a young athlete named Giavanni Ruffin who plays American Football for East Carolina College but is striving to make it professionally in the NFL. The videos are called "How bad do you want it" and "How bad do you want it part 2" and are voiced over by renowned motivational speaker and author Eric Thomas.

I have written this book as a plan of action, rather than a theory or a set of background information that requires you to struggle to extract meaningful actions from. I have written this as a coach, keeping it simple and keeping it real. At the end of each chapter, I have provided a very brief summary of what you need to do to get to the top, in simple steps. Not everyone will need or want do every single one, nevertheless, the more you do, the more chance you have of becoming successful and reaching the top of your game.

I sincerely hope this book gets you to where you want to be, and I wish you all the best for your journey.

If you have questions along the way or you need advice, then there is a link at the end of this book to a forum that I host at newpersonalbest.co.uk/ where you can ask them, or just visit to post your dreams or tell me how you are getting along.

Part 1 - Prepare to be Great

CHAPTER 1

IT ALL STARTS WITH A DREAM

"A journey of a thousand miles must begin with a single step." – Laozi (Zhou Dynasty – 6th century BC) Founder of the Taoist philosophy.

As you read this book there will be chapters and statements about what you have to do and what you have to go through to achieve success in sport, as a person and as an athlete. It all starts with a dream.

"Don't put a limit on anything. The more you dream the farther you get" – Michael Phelps (1985-) US Swimmer, the most decorated Olympian of all time.

The First Step

Being "a dreamer" has negative connotations. The moniker suggests someone who is far away or "off in the clouds". People ridicule dreamers as being unrealistic because dreams do not come true. In some cases, dreams are acceptable as long as you do not pursue them. Worse still, your dreams are acceptable to others as long as they are unrealistic because they don't have to be taken seriously. As soon as they become realistic or achievable you can be seen to be arrogant, or boastful in pursuing your dream.

Being open about a dream can make you become the subject of teasing, or worse, bullying. Often, people tend to hide their dreams. This chapter will help you develop your dream and share it, whilst guarding against the negative influences of others.

"A superior man is modest in his speech, but exceeds in his actions" – Confucius (551-479BC), Chinese Philosopher

This chapter is the start of your journey to success. It is about separating yourself from other people's reality. Their reality is not your reality. Their success and, more importantly, their lack of success is not yours. Their jealousy cannot become your limitation. Their lack of a dream should not detract from your dream. You need to separate yourself from the negativity of others. Isolate yourself from the performance of others. Use their story to fuel your dream, not detract from it. Someone else's failure does not mean you will fail. It means you should learn from their failure and use that to drive you, to make fewer mistakes, to take a different path, to work harder.

"Do just once what others say you can't do and you will never pay attention to their limitations again" – James R Cook (1728-1779) Author

Pick the right dream

"The starting point of all achievement is desire. Weak desire brings weak results" – Napolean Hill (1883-1970) Author

You are going to have to work very hard for success, go through pain, suffering, and sacrifice to achieve success. To do this you need to be clear what dream you are chasing and what it means to you.

The first principle is to dream big.

"Your dream should not be out of sight, but it should be out of reach"- Anita Defrantz (1952-) Olympic

Rower and member of the International Olympic Committee

If you play Football, your dream could be to play in the Premier League. If it is Tennis it could be to play at Wimbledon. Competing in the Olympics, or playing in a major tournament in Golf are both goals you should be prepared to set for yourself. Whatever your sport, your dream should involve getting to the top echelon of that sport. Try to define your success by how other people would view your sport. A general consensus of what is successful is a good indicator of actual success. Do not be fooled though: other people's opinions of your chances of success are not the factor here. Other people do not have to mitigate their opinions of what is realistic, because they can be objective. If you asked them what they would see as success in a particular sport, they would tell you; the Tour de France, Wimbledon, Olympics, Premiership Rugby, Premier League. It would be the top echelon of the sport.

"Any man who selects a goal in life which can be fully achieved has already defined his own limitations"- Cavett Robert (1907-1997) Founder of the National Speakers Association

You need to dream of that level of success to engage you in the work that you will need to do to get there. There are no shortcuts, no overnight successes, but on the other hand don't allow yourself or anyone else to impose limitations. As the US Cycling Coach, Carl Cantrell says, you cannot achieve more than you think you can. If you think you can't achieve something, then you can be sure that you can't.

"The greatest danger for most of us is not that we aim too high and miss it, but we aim too low and reach it" – Michelangelo (1475-1564) Sculptor, painter, architect, poet and engineer

The first thing you need to do is define your dream. Everything else is built on this - every drop of sweat shed, every repetition completed, every moment of pain endured - so you need to make sure you have put some effort into this stage. The better you define it, the more it will endure and drive you. It need not be complicated; it just has to be clear.

"Sometimes the biggest problem is in your head. You have got to believe" – Jack Nicklaus (1940-) 3rd all time PGA Tour Winning Golfer

There are a number of mistakes people make with their dream. Usually these involve getting the 'What' (this is the dream) mixed up with the 'Why', the 'Who' and the

'How'. To avoid these errors, lets start with some examples of the things that are not your dream.

The 'Who' is a common error. "I want to be the next David Beckham" or the next "Andy Murray" or the next "insert your own hero here", and this can seem like a reasonable place to start, but being someone else is not the right dream for you. For one thing you do not really know who they are, you only know their public persona. They have flaws, fears, problems, and issues just like all of us. The biggest problem in terms of defining your dream this way is that they are not you and you are not them. The trials and tribulations that they have endured to get to the top are not the same as yours. Their history is not your history. What if they are not what you think they are? What if you base your dream on someone else, with their human frailties, and they fall from grace? What if you wanted to be the next Lance Armstrong, Oscar Pistorius or Tyson Gay? Would your dream still be alive now? You cannot base your dream on being someone else because, ultimately, your dream is not theirs and they might let you down.

Do not try to be the next anyone. Be the first you. You are unique, your journey is unique. Why would you want to be someone else? Aim to be better. It is perfectly reasonable to emulate someone else, to be inspired by one of the greats. This is covered in Chapter 2. You can want to achieve what they have achieved. That is a good way to define your dream. But do not just decide to be someone else, because you will end up disappointed.

It isn't the 'Why'

The ‘Why’ is an important one and will be covered in a later chapter, but, for now, for the purposes of understanding how to define your dream, this is about where your drive comes from. It may be getting away from a situation, pulling yourself from poverty, making a better life for your family. These are all good examples of why you are motivated to achieve your dream. But they are not your dream. The ‘Why’ is not the ‘What’ and the ‘Why’ is not enough. It is a facet of the desire, the drive, but the dream has to be much more than that.

It isn’t the ‘How’

Another mistake is to confuse the ‘How’ with the dream. This is mixing the journey with the destination. Try an example. “I want to have the hardest shot in the English Premier League”. But to what end? David Hirst is an old hero of mine and when I was young I watched him play football for Sheffield Wednesday. Hirst hit a 114mph thunderbolt against Arsenal for Sheffield Wednesday on 16 September 1996, a record which still stands at the time of writing as the hardest shot in the Premier League, some 17 years later. The shot hit the bar and Sheffield Wednesday lost the game 4-1. The moral is that even in the shortest term, the accolade meant nothing. Because Hirst never claimed a place in the England Football Team, he never really achieved the greatness he was destined for that some of his contemporaries did, particularly Alan Shearer OBE. This is no criticism of David Hirst - as I have stated he was my hero when I was young, but he was plagued by injury. The point is that having the hardest shot is not the end in itself, but it might be a means to the end.

This might have been for Hirst what sales people would call a USP – a Unique Selling Point, but it isn't the whole package. The end is the success which would have been, for Hirst, the England number 9 shirt. So, do not define your dream by what your selling point will be - fastest serve, longest drive, longest throw-in or whatever. These might be how you get noticed, or what you use to sell yourself, but the end result that you are trying to achieve, your success, is something different. In the remainder of this book I will guide you in the 'How', but first you need to understand the 'What' your dream is.

'What' is your dream?

I have covered what your dream isn't, so now let's cover what it is.

What are you really dreaming about? It should be simple and not too specific. "I will compete in the Premier League (or at Wimbledon or in the Olympics)". It is that simple. That is your dream. KISS – Keep It Simple, Stupid.

"If you always put limits on everything you do, physical or anything else, it will spread into your life. There are no limits. There are only plateaus and you must not stay there, you must go beyond them." – Bruce Lee (1940-1973) Chinese-American Martial Artist, Actor and Filmaker

Craig Pickering was an Olympic 100m sprinter, and was on track to represent Team GB at the 2012 Olympics until injury struck and he lost his funding. Pickering then focussed on bobsleigh and was selected for the Winter Olympics in Sochi in 2014 becoming only the 8th British athlete to achieve selection in both summer and winter Olympics. His dream was clear, he wanted to win Olympic medals and when one door closed, he opened a new one.

If you wanted to play for Chelsea and ended up playing for Manchester United, would you turn away? Or if you wanted to play for the Harlequins at Rugby Union and ended up playing for Bath would you think you had not achieved your dream? So your dream need not be specific. If it helps you to dream of wearing a specific shirt or competing at a specific event, then by all means do so, but understand that you do not have to hang your entire dream on it. Your "what" might be a feeling. Christian Malcolm, the Team GB sprinter described to me the feeling of the 2012 Olympic games for him. "We didn't see much of the games beforehand, we were in a camp in Portugal for the first part and then once we arrived, we were in the Olympic Village and doing our own thing, preparing for our events. So the first real experience I had was walking out into the stadium for my heat. 80,000 people clapping and cheering was just amazing. Then when they announced the people in my heat, they announced lane 1, lane 2, and then on lane 3, which was mine, this huge roar went up, it was deafening. I was trying to focus get in my zone and the javelin was going on at the same time so I just thought it was someone doing a big throw. So I looked up at the big screen and there I was, the roar was for me! Incredible! I've never experienced anything like it".

That is a dream worth striving for right there.

Bringing Your Dream to Life

So once you have your dream, what then? You need to spend some time on it, nurture it, make it live, speak it into existence, commit to it. So how do you do this? First you have to write it down, make sure you are happy with it, that it inspires you, and that it is big enough to push you through the sacrifice and the pain. Make sure it can stand the test of time and that it will be the same 10 years from now. Make sure that you will be able to keep getting up after being knocked down because you want it badly enough. Once you have it, find a place where you can spend some quiet time nurturing your dream and then stick what you have written in that place, somewhere like the back of your bedroom door, or on the mirror in the bathroom, in the garden shed, or somewhere that you train. Anywhere that you can take a few minutes out of your schedule to spend time to remember what you are doing all this for, what you are striving for.

Now take the time to imagine yourself where you want to be. Think what it would feel like, what it would sound like, the smells and the sights. Make it live, make it real. Better yet, if you have been close to that place as a spectator, take yourself back there. Do not just remember it - experience it again. Imagine what it would be like being on that team, in that place, being where you want to be. Once you have yourself there, stare at that dream, burn it into your mind with all those emotions and feelings that you have just brought to life. Each time you come here they will be brighter, more vivid and as you get closer, have better experiences, you can make this image even more detailed so you know exactly what you are working for.

To Share or Not To Share?

The next part of making your dream come alive is the trickiest and will change from person to person, or from athlete to athlete. It is about other people knowing about your dream. This is where your support system of family and friends come into play. How will they react? Will they be 100% behind you, or will they laugh and belittle your dream or your chances of success? Some people feed off negativity by setting out to prove the doubters wrong, but others will be completely crushed by it, especially if the negativity comes from someone you trust or respect. On the one hand, sharing your dream so others can encourage and support you is very important. However, if the person being negative is trusted, like a best friend, a coach, a teacher or a parent then this can be catastrophic, so you need to take care with your choice and so you should follow my guidance below.

"Go after your dream, no matter how unattainable others think it is" – Linda Mastrandrea (Present) US Paralympian and Author.

So, first and foremost before you share your dream you need to consider who you will share it with. How are they likely to react? Be realistic. If they are usually negative or critical, they are unlikely to suddenly change this just because you are pursuing your dream, no matter how much you want them to. Proving people wrong is alright if you do not need their support or their opinion does not matter too much.

You need to be honest with yourself on how they will respond and be honest with yourself on how you will react to their response. Remember, your dream is out of reach, so most realistic and pragmatic people will try to be just that, realistic or pragmatic, which means they will try and get you to mitigate what you are aiming for, to lower your sights. They do not want you to be hurt or disappointed. They will not understand that you are fully aware of the probability of achieving your dream and the setbacks you can expect along the way. They will try to protect you, and this is normal, but they will kill your dream with kindness. Be strong, these people are being supportive so do not dismiss them, convince them, get them on your side. Make sure they understand that you are fully aware of the implications of pursuing your dream and that you are prepared to work for it.

"Tell everyone what you want to do and someone will want to help you do it" – W. Clement Stone (1902-2002) Businessman, philanthropist and author.

Dealing with Negativity

Not everyone will be positive; some will be jealous and derogatory. Some will actively try to prevent you from pursuing your dream. In some cases, all you can do with these people is to ignore them. At best, you can cut this negativity from your support circle, find new friends who perhaps share your interest in your chosen sport. This is not possible if the person is a sibling or a parent though, and, in this case, you have to build a support network that can overcome this. Share your dream with your training group, or others who share your passion. Find an online forum, find like-minded athletes. You might be surprised by how many share a similar dream but just do not talk about it for the same reason that you don't, through embarrassment or misplaced modesty.

Understand that wanting to be successful is not immodest or arrogant. You have a dream and you are prepared to work for it. Having belief is not the same as being arrogant, but negative people will see it that way.

Mutual Support

Once you have your support network or group, and when you have shared your dream with them, then use them. Friends, teammates, and family are there for you as you are there for them. Be prepared to give to them what they are giving to you. Support each other. They may have completely different motivations and dreams, but if they are supporting you then you must support them in turn. However, for your part, be open with what you might want from them. If you need them to pick you up when you get knocked down then tell them beforehand. If you want them to remind you about your dream when you are feeling low, remind you what you have done so far, how far you have come, then tell them that is what you want. It isn't needy to want encouragement one in a while.

Summary

The steps to take away from this chapter are as follows:

1. Define your dream. Identify what it is you want to achieve, keep it simple, out of reach but not out of sight.

2. Write your dream down. Make it real by speaking it into existence.

3. Stick what you have written down somewhere you can spend time with it.

4. Make your dream live in your mind. The sights, sounds, smells and feelings.

5. Identify who will support you. Be realistic about what you expect from them.

6. Share your dream. Get the support for your journey.

CHAPTER 2

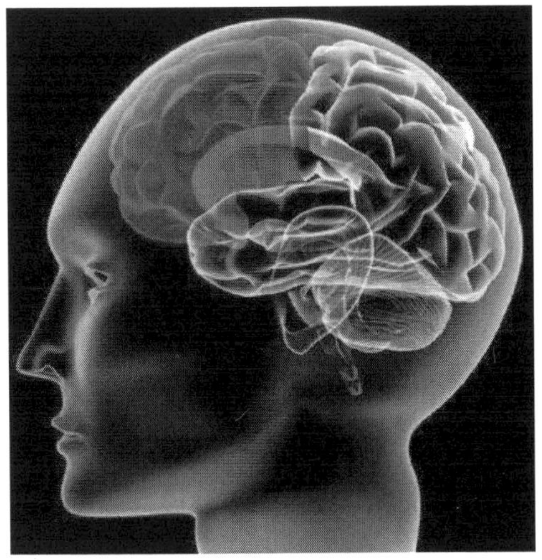

BEING AN INTELLIGENT ATHLETE

There comes a point when you realise you might be good at a sport. It might be that someone else tells you or you might just be obviously better than your peers. Once you have this realisation and you have developed your dream of becoming a top sportsman or sportswoman (and have read Chapter 1 of course), then you need to work out what it takes to be great, because being good is not enough.

There are many people who are good but did not make it, and you do not want to be one of those. There is more to being elite than being technically proficient. You have to be able to deliver a performance time and time again, all season long. You have to be able to handle different levels of competition, different styles and different levels of pressure. You have to be able to compete. Sport is competition, which means you have to beat other people, either as an individual or as a team. Not only do you have to perform during each competition, you have to perform consistently over a number of rounds, events, or even a season.

To truly understand what it takes to be great, you have to be a student of your sport. Learn about what it takes to achieve greatness in that sport and how to play the game, not just execute the performance. You have to be an intelligent athlete. There are many more facets to sport than what you see as a young athlete. You have to search them out, find out what they are and implement them into your sporting make-up.

The best way to understand this, and quite an enjoyable way, is to watch the film Any Given Sunday. This film is about an American Football team and has a thread on exactly this topic. The journey of the young quarterback Willie Beamen, played by Jamie Foxx, is exactly what this chapter is about. Midway through the film, his coach Tony D'Amato, played by Al Pacino, has Beamen over for dinner to try to explain to him this very principle, about understanding the team, understanding the game. Watching it will help you understand what you need to do. Beamen's transformation from the beginning of the film to the end is extreme, (this is an entertainment film after all), so you see a condensed version of the 'before' and 'after'.

Know the Rules

The first principle is to understand the rules of your sport. This is such a fundamental requirement that it seems too obvious to mention, but there are so many athletes who do not know all the rules of their sport. Kids tend to drift into sports, playing "pick-up" games in the street, in the playground or in the park. There are few rules in these games. They then drift into more organised sport and learn enough, by osmosis, to play the sport, but the idiosyncrasies and nuances of the sport often pass kids by. Coaches do not really take the time to explain the rules, it tends to be assumed. But, in my many years in sport, I have known that the greater proportion of coaches do not know all the rules themselves. Some people will think this is not that important, but we all understand that knowledge is power. If nothing else, you have an advantage if you know how to avoid breaking the rules. Knowing the rules also allows you options and to know how you can adapt your play when necessary.

"90% of the game is played above the shoulders." - Jim Geddes, Baseball Pitcher Chicago White Sox (1949 - present)

England's cricket team won one of the sport's greatest prizes, 'The Ashes', with a tactic called

'Bodyline' or 'fast leg theory' in their 1932/33 series. Team captain Douglas Jardine and fast-bowler Harold Larwood were vilified in Australia for pushing the boundaries of the rules. This tactic involved crowding the batsman with fielders and then bowling very fast high-bouncing deliveries into his body so that his only viable options were to be hit by the ball or play defensively to protect himself. However, the defensive shots were all within the range of the close-in fielders leading to an inevitable dismissal of the batsman. This was all within the rules, but seen to be unfair by many. Whatever people's opinion of Larwood and Jardine, their team won and they did it within the rules of the game.

While this is an extreme example, the principle stands that knowing all the rules is an advantage in all sports. As well as the general rules for a particular sport, you should also be aware that different events or competitions have different rules as well.

As an example, sprinting is a relatively simple sport with few rules, and getting into the sport does not necessarily require a knowledge of those rules, you just have to run fast. But understanding the starter's commands and how long you are allowed to take to do things (for example how long the starter is allowed to hold the athletes in 'set' position) is very important. The athlete who knows that the starter will not call "set" until all the athletes are completely motionless in the "on your marks position" can stay in motion until they are ready. This is why if you watch a sprint race on television you will see the athletes swaying from side to side. They use this to control the point at which the starter calls “set”. Add to this that knowing the time you can afford to take to get into the take your marks position means that an opponent who rushes into position could be in this compact stance for a considerable period longer than you before going into “set”, and this can give you an advantage. In the 400m, an indoor race is completely different to an outdoor one as it has a ‘break’ out of lane, the only individual sprint event that does. Although the distance is the same as the outdoor, the race tactics are completely different. Knowing when to break, how the break works, and being able to command a lane that other athletes are in are all critical to avoid disqualification and in controlling the race.

Lastly, doping rules are vitally important and start surprisingly early. Knowing what is and is not a banned substance is critical, as ignorance is no defence. Failing a drug test would be devastating and potentially career-ending, but can happen through something as seemingly innocuous as an over-the-counter hay fever medicine. Knowing the rules so that you do not break them is as important as knowing them so that you can use them to your advantage. It is not just the rules, but also the application of them that is also important. The Scottish Skier Alain Baxter was stripped of his bronze medal from the Winter Olympics in Salt Lake City in 2002 after a positive drugs test. On appeal it was found that the positive test was caused by a common “off the shelf” cold remedy, a Vicks inhaler, which had different ingredients in the US to those in the UK. The stimulant discovered was an inactive version of a banned stimulant. However, even though the court for arbitration for sport accepted his explanation, both his ban and loss of medal still stood! In a more recent example, Welsh Athletics duo Rhys Williams and Gareth Warburton were suspended just before the 2014 Commonwealth Games after testing positive for banned substances. It appears (the hearing will be held after publication of this book) that this will be proven to be from a contaminated batch of product from their supplement supplier. They will, however, still have served an effective ban, even if their defense is accepted and will have missed the Commonwealth Games.

A salutary lesson. From a more positive perspective, knowing what is legal as well is beneficial. Creatine and Caffeine were originally banned but have recently been made legal and are now widely used. Staying current with all the changes and updates gives you an advantage.

How Sport Works

The second principle is to know how your sport works. If we continue to follow our sprinting example, the running of the race is the obvious part, but what does it take to get to an elite level? As you have your dream firmly in place, we can consider a national level event for this purpose. First, you have to qualify. How do you qualify: are there specific events or specific times? In this case it is based on time, but the time has to be set in a particular qualifying period. So knowing when this is will allow you to manage your training. Then there is the target event itself. How is it run? How many rounds? Are they on one day, over two days, or more?

In sprinting there are two factors to consider in the events themselves. Usually there is a qualifying round, and then semi-finals, followed by a final. Energy needs to be conserved for the final, but not at the expense of failing to qualify. How fast do you need to run to qualify through the rounds? Information from previous events can tell you a lot about this. In many cases, the times at national events with multiple rounds do not tend to be where personal best performances are run. By the time athletes get to the final they are already fatigued. What this tells you is that being the fastest is not enough; tactics through the rounds is also a factor.

I recently heard the Dutch National Relays coach Wiggert Thunnisen speak at a conference about how the Dutch team had had extraordinary success at relays with their absolute understanding that the time it takes to get the baton round the track is more important than the individual sprint times. If the Dutch sprinters raced in individual races then the sum of their times would suggest that the Dutch team would be way down the relay rankings compared to other countries. However, they consistently win international medals with both men's and women's relays by getting the baton round faster so that the speed of the baton from start to finish is maximised from their individual performances. A simple idea, the time the baton takes to travel around the track, has been exploited and executed to amazing results.

"What makes you successful is to never quit learning." - David Cutcliffe, Head US Football Coach at Duke University (1954 - present)

It is clear from these examples that there is more to the sport than meets the eye, but do not be fooled into writing this off because the examples here may not be from your sport. Your sport, whatever it is, will have equivalent pathways and routes that you will need to understand.

Sport Governance

The third principle is to learn how the governance works. What this means is learn about your club, who is in it, who can help you, how can they help you? What about the governing body (or bodies) of your sport? Is there funding or opportunities available that you can use?

Most people give no consideration to how everything in their sport happens. I was no different when I played sports. I turned up where I was told to, did what I was asked to and then went home until the next time. I gave no consideration to how much work goes on behind the scenes and to what was involved in making all the things happen to allow me to participate. If nothing else, an appreciation of the people that do the work for you is useful. Selfishly, if you have a coach, then appreciating how much effort they put in on your behalf is going to mean that, when the chips are down, the coach will be happy to be on your side because he/she knows that they are appreciated. You also need to understand the limitations of the structure you are in and if this is holding you back.

You are on your own path, no-one else's and everyone else has their own agenda whether it impacts you positively or negatively. Understanding this allows better informed decisions. Most likely, your coach works in a club structure. This puts specific restrictions on him/her. This may be in terms of competition, or financing, team selection or many other restrictions. So, does your team have a sponsor whose son/daughter plays for the team? Do they get preferential treatment? For that matter, does your coach have a son/daughter that plays for the team and do they get preferential treatment? Coaches also have a private life and this can also create restrictions. Is your training quantity and timing based on ideal conditions or are they because your coach has other commitments. This is not a criticism of any coach (of which I am one) but the majority of coaches are volunteers and are not at the beck and call of athletes. Understanding what the restrictions and limitations are allows you to create your personal ideal scenario. Just because your coach can't be at training, does not mean you can't. Will he/she set you additional sessions? Are you allowed to compete at different events, with a different club even?

Pushing Boundaries

Finally, while you are still developing, you need to try things out and see how rules are applied. Test the boundaries in an event where it doesn't matter so you know where they are when it does. If you get disqualified in an unimportant race, you will know how far you can push. If you attempt different strategies to see how they work in a game then you'll have them in the armoury when you need them. When I suggest trying things out and pushing boundaries, I am referring to the rules of how the sport is played, such as the false-start rule. Do not, under any circumstances, attempt to test the boundaries of the doping rules. By all means, if a substance is completely legal, then try it (with a doctors advice), but if you are unsure then don't take any risks. The gains of supplements are so marginal that it is better to be safe than sorry.

Summary

If you want to be a top-level athlete, then you must understand your sport. Don't just turn up and play like everyone else.

1. Learn the rules
2. Learn the sport
3. Learn the governance and structure
4. Try things out!

CHAPTER 3

LEARNING FROM THE GREATS

To be elite, you need to figure out what it takes to get there. You need to know how long it takes, how hard it is, how to go about it. You also need to recognise the character traits that the people who reach the top in sport have. This is not immediately obvious but in my experience over the years, and latterly in my research for this book, I see the same thread going through all the people at the top of their sport. But, before I get to that, it is worth understanding the things that the greats in sport do not have in common.

"Winners imagine their dreams first. They want it with all their heart & expect it to come true. There's no other way to live." -Joe Montana (1956-) American Football Player and 4-time Superbowl Winner

How was it for you?

Firstly, there is no blueprint for what a person should be like physically to get to the top. If you accept stereotypes and obstacles like this, then you will simply confirm the stereotype. In his book The Sports Gene, David Epstein identifies common genetic codes for people who succeed in different sports, but these are not rules. There are always exceptions and these mean that we don't fully understand yet who can and who can't achieve an elite level. We only know the common features of the ones that have been tested, but sport and genetics are too complex to let them get in the way just yet. Remember this – Usain Bolt, the fastest man on earth and winner of the 'double-triple' winning all 3 sprint gold medals at two subsequent Olympics, is "too tall" to be a 100m sprinter. That was the perceived wisdom of many experts. Tall sprinters cannot accelerate adequately due to their long biomechanical levers. No-one remembered to tell Bolt and he proved that you should not be constrained by what other people think. US High Jumper Jessie Williams is one of the shortest and heaviest athletes in his discipline at elite level. Giving away four inches to Olympic Champion Ivan Ukhov and carrying 28 pounds more weight did not stop Williams from becoming World Champion in 2011. The stereotypes tell you what the 'norm' is, nothing more. Great athletes are exceptional and exceptional means they are the exceptions to the norm, even among elite athletes.

"Do not let what you cannot do interfere with what you can do." - John Wooden, legendary US College Football Coach, won an unprecedented 10 NCAA Championships in 12 years (1910-2010)

Secondly, there is no background that allows better performance in sport. It is not environmental, nor is it financial. There are as many examples of rich people making it as there are poor people. There are as many examples of athletes whose parents have no background in sport as there are parents that have a history. You can find examples to support any theory because there is no real common factor for a successful background. Obviously, if you want to be a professional skier, it helps if you live close to somewhere that has regular snow, but this is about opportunity not background. If you want an extreme, great fun example then watch Disney's 'Cool Runnings' starring the late John Candy. This is based on the true story of the Jamaican bobsleigh team competing in the Winter Olympics for the first time.

Thirdly, at a developing level and beyond the basics, facilities are not that important. What this means is that if you are a track athlete, then having an indoor facility to train in is nice, but in itself does not have causality to success. The UK has some wonderful indoor facilities and hi tech performance centres, which is great, but this has not improved their track performance. Most Jamaican sprinters, until very recently, did not have access to a track and therefore they trained on grass. Wilton Peart, a 38-year-old Jamaican 100 meters runner, was once a professional athlete and he believes that running on grass strengthens the muscles. Peart points out that Bolt also started out on grass at William Knibb High School, which he attended until he was 18. In fact, Jamaica has only five all-weather synthetic tracks. Poverty, Peart notes, is a great motivator.

Reading about the athletes who have made it in your sport, and researching through TV, radio or the internet, will give you great inspiration. No-one has an easy ride, there are no escalators to the top, everyone has to take the stairs. There are setbacks and diversions. There is rarely a straight route. Knowing that this is common and how others overcame their difficulties is necessary to help you through when you hit yours. This does not have to be a chore or some major project. It should be done over time, as part of an interest in your sport. If you do not like reading, get DVDs, use the internet and find old interviews that you can listen to; whatever works for you. If you can, see if you can contact them. You might be surprised how many sports stars are willing to talk to you if they have the time. If you are still at school, combine it with an assignment and get the best of both worlds.

If you are slightly outside the norm for your sport, find the people who made it that have been or are similar to you. Find out what they did, how they went about it. If they managed it then so can you, and there is little point in reinventing the wheel. If you really want inspiration, take a look at the Paralympians who do your sport. See how they overcome their adversities. The 'Meet the Superhumans' advert before the 2012 Paralympic Games is the most inspirational thing I have ever seen.

Once you are familiar with your own sport, cast your net wider. Look for other sportsmen and women who have achieved great things. Get a range of different sports, men and women, from different eras. You will start to see the consistency between them all. You will understand what you have to do and you will find that you are probably already doing a lot of it. If you love sport, what you need to do won't be a chore. Every waking hour is either playing for fun, playing competitively, or thinking about playing. You will realise that, when it comes down to it, this is what you need to continue to do. The level you are doing it at will change, the difficulty will change, the professionalism and the quality will change, but, fundamentally, you are playing or planning continuously and consistently, and everything else plays second fiddle.

The tough parts of the sport are external to the physical act of participating. Once you understand the greats, you will see that this rings true throughout, that the fundamental love for playing their sport wins out through any adversity, winning and losing, injury and circumstance. They are all part of the game and, when you understand that, you will have a great opportunity to become successful.

So, it is not background, it is not stereotypes and it is not facilities, so what is it? Simply put, it is about desire. Desire, commitment and sacrifice; although the latter two come from the first. The athletes that make it to the top in any sport do so because they are fully committed to success in that sport (although some divert, they just become fully committed to a different sport). They are the athletes that are not just playing the sport, they are pursuing a course of action that is leading them ever on to better and better things. To understand what this really means needs some research. The examples that I will give in this chapter only scratch the surface to provide an indication, to show you what you are looking for. The desire is a conscious decision, a polarisation of your life as an athlete to achieving your dream, as the people you are researching did.

"Success comes from focussing the full power of all you are on what you have a burning desire to achieve." – Wilfred A Peterson (1900-1995) US Author

Read about athletes in your sport and register what they say, in autobiographies, in interviews when they talk about how hard they work and what they have to achieve. Watch TV programmes that document training and look for the sacrifices they make, not just the training they do.

These are small examples, but Victoria Pendleton CBE, many times World and Olympic champion in various track cycling events, couldn't wear high heels or go dancing because of the chance of injury to her legs. Andrew 'Freddie' Flintoff MBE, Ashes winning cricketer, talked in the Sky TV program 'From Lords to the Ring' of being bullied because he was the only one in his school who played cricket instead of football. The wife of Sir Bradley Wiggins, Tour de France and many time Olympic medallist, talks of him being completely absent from his family during preparation for major championships and being unable to lift a suitcase into the boot of the car for fear of injury. Former England footballer Alan Shearer OBE left home at the age of 17 to move to Southampton to play football. At the age of 12, Tennis champion Novak Djokovic left home in Serbia to attend the Pilić Tennis academy in Oberschleißheim, Germany. This is over and above the friends, parties, birthdays, holidays and all the other small but inevitable and incessant sacrifices that great athletes make continuously that I will cover in more detail in Chapter 6.

Most importantly, do not look for the differences between you and the people you are aspiring to match. That way will lead you to reason that they are different to you and eventually you may decide that you cannot achieve what they achieve. Instead do two things, whether you are researching people within your sport or in other sports.

Common Ground

First, look for the commonalities. While some athletes are successful in their sport from a young age, this is rarely the case. They may be involved in the sport but seemingly burst through late, or are successful in a different sport at junior level and then switch sports. On the other hand, there are countless examples of "morning stars" that shine brightly at U11, U13 and even U15 age groups but then burn themselves out and disappear forever. I will cover this in detail in Chapter 9.

So, some athletes stand out from an early age but many don't. You need to look into who they played for, when they were recognised to have real potential, who recognised them, how did it happen? What obstacles were in their way on their journey?

"If you're trying to achieve, there will be roadblocks. I've had them, everybody has had them" – Michael Jordan (1963-) NBA Basketball player and businessman, many believe to be the greatest basketball player of all time.

Vive la difference!

Secondly, look at what they did that is different to their peers. What was the extra mile that made the difference? Get a feel for it. Go your own path, but use their journey to guide you. Examples include England footballer David Beckham OBE staying behind after training to do extra work on his ball control and free kicks; Cyclist Mark Cavendish MBE used to let the tyres down on his mountain bike when he was playing at racing his mates to make it harder, or practised by riding hard against the wind. Here is England Rugby Union Number 10 Toby

Flood describing predecessor Jonny Wilkinson OBE to The Independent newspaper. “When I was starting out, the thing that struck me most about Jonny was his desire. It seemed oxymoronic at the time: the world’s best player, training harder than everyone else. But to see someone blessed with that ability showing such endeavour, such a determination to leave no stone unturned in the quest to be better…it showed us what we could be like if we followed his example.”

It could be anything and your extra mile will be different, but get an idea how it works, find it. for your journey and start doing it.

"Champions aren't made in gyms. Champions are made from something they have deep inside them: A desire, a dream, a vision. They have to have last-minute stamina, they have to be a little faster, they have to have the skill and the will. But the will must be stronger than the skill." – Muhammad Ali (1942-) Former professional boxer and considered by mane as the greatest heavyweight of all time.

Will to win = Hate to lose

Another thing that the greats have in common that comes up consistently along with their desire is that all of them hate losing. This does not make them bad losers necessarily (although many will be tarred with this brush and of course, some are) but it does mean it bothers them more than their peers and they will push hard to make sure they do everything they can to prevent it happening again – this is a fundamental cause of improvement. Lastly they all tend to be competitive. Not just in their sport, that is a given, but in almost everything. It does not matter whether it is another sport, playing cards, exams or any other feature or activity. The greats are usually described as “true competitors”.

A lot of them excelled at more than one sport. If you look at the character, you can probably predict that if they had been born elsewhere or in different circumstances, then they would have been great at a different sport. A cyclist may have been a skier, an American Football quarterback may have been a cricketer. It is their athletic and psychological attributes, the same attributes that have been highlighted in this chapter, that make them great. Their sport is just the one they happen to have chosen (or that ‘chose’ them). Look for these attributes in yourself. If you have the desire, are competitive, and hate losing then you are half way there.

Summary

While your journey is your own, there is a lot to learn from how other people have made their journey. People that are like you and people that are different to you. You will find that there are no common backgrounds, opportunities or routes.

1. Find people in sport who inspire you or whose achievements you want to emulate (it does not have to be in your own sport).

2. Read about them, watch or listen to interviews, read their autobiography, learn from them.

3. Look at how they got to the top, what they are doing, how committed they are and were.

4. Apply what you have learned to your own approach.

CHAPTER 4

PREPARING YOURSELF FOR SUCCESS

This chapter is about how to prepare yourself to make the most of everything you have got. It is about building a career around your dream that is wider than the singular focus you have, but starting that preparation from the outset. This is about preparing the icing on the cake, or maybe even the cherry on the icing. It will help facilitate the other areas that will be covered in the rest of the book. It will also help for the future after your competitive career is over. I have found over the years that the things described have always worked in one form or another, sometimes not as I would expect them to. This chapter is not about specifically planning for things, it is about creating opportunities and preparing yourself to exploit them.

How to create your opportunities

If you are a gardener, then you grow things by preparing the ground and planting seeds. Then every so often, you pop back and do a bit of watering, weeding and so on. At the end something might grow so you have a crop and sometimes it does not (in my case with gardening this is the most common result). Now, if you are a good gardener, you can probably predict how many seeds you need to grow a certain amount of crop, what to plant and when to plant it. But in life, you can't see far enough into the future to plan everything, especially when you are highly focused on a goal of becoming an elite sportsman or woman. You do not really want to think too much about what to do when you retire, never mind what you will do if something happens that prevents you from reaching the top.

In business, a good risk manager will have contingencies and fall back plans for all sorts of eventualities, but this is too exhausting and time consuming for most. Nevertheless, what you can do is take a scattergun approach because to grow a large oak you might have to plant many acorns. Some will not grow, some will grow and then, because you have not paid attention to them, will wither and die, some will grow well and you will never know because you have never looked at them again. But some will grow and be there when you need them.

Enough metaphors, what does all this mean? It means you have to make an effort with everyone you meet. Decide how you want to be viewed and be your own brand all the time. You will have thousands upon thousands of interactions over the course of your sporting life and every single one of them may be able to help you at some point in the future. If you then add in the connections and networks that they have, then you are potentially connected to someone that could make a real difference to you. Remember this; if you become a professional in most sports, you will need sponsors. You could be meeting some of the people that will connect you to these sponsors from a young age. How do you portray yourself to them? This is not only about how you act on the pitch or on the track, on the course or in the ring. It is about how you act with your competitors when you win and lose, with officials and supporters.

"In order to be the best anything in life, you have to be the best YOU first!" - Khadevis Robinson, 4-time US Champion at 800m (1976 - present)

What you have to realise is that sponsors pay money to people that they can relate to, who will represent them, and who will not let them down with bad publicity. They will also want something in return such as speaking to their employees, attending in-house company events, or even giving them media support. Think what kind of person you would look for if you wanted someone to do that? A sponsor is basically employing you to represent them. They will not be employing a stroppy teenager, and do not think for one second that they will base their decisions on "Any publicity is good publicity".

To be marketable, you need to be able to speak eloquently, to be able to hold a conversation with a variety of people and be able to talk coherently about your sport. You also need to be someone who can engage other people. Jessica Ennis CBE, 2012 Olympic heptathlon champion, is a shining example of a marketable athlete.

Do your schoolwork

You will have heard multiple times, probably from parents, about how schoolwork is important. You may feel that it is not as important as sport, but not only is it important in its own right, the way you approach it is also important. The first reason is that you need to earn money whether you are a sportsman/woman or not. The next section looks at different ways to approach that as a sportsman or woman, but being uneducated won't help any of them.

Ultimately, do not think of education as a contingency. It is a fundamental part of being an athlete and you have to approach every task you do with absolute focus and determination to succeed, even if you spend less time on it than you would your sport. You cannot just be 'that kind of athlete' you have to be 'that kind of person' so that your approach is the same in everything that you do.

"We are what we repeatedly do. Excellence then is not an act, but a habit" - Aristotle (384 BC-342 BC) Greek Philosopher

The second reason is that in almost every sport other than football your best opportunity will come from attending University. Universities generally have better facilities than any other sports clubs and they have a greater range of supported sports clubs than those that you will find locally. You will have the range of equipment you need, such as the best gym equipment, indoor training facilities, and coaches. You will often also have a high degree of flexibility in your time to allow you to train at better and more regular intervals.

You must push yourself forward and create the opportunities for yourself that others rely on luck for. This is one of those situations where finding the right course at the right University will give you a phenomenal push forward in your sporting journey.

Being a sporty person may mean you do not see yourself as academically talented enough to attend a University, but talent is earned, whether it is sport or school. It is a result of the level **and quality** of work you put in. If you put the quality of effort into your school work necessary then you will be capable of achieving the grades that you need. Do not write it off through lack of interest. If you are a sports person, then you are interested in sport. You need to be an intelligent athlete. So go to University so that someone will teach you about sport. Do a PE qualification and they will teach you the rules. Do Sports Science and they will teach you how your training program works and why.

Going to University is not necessarily a pre-requisite for becoming an elite sportsman, but it is a guaranteed way to have the opportunity to train regularly and with the best facilities. You may get picked up by a professional team before then and get that anyway without the distractions, but if you are still at school it would be foolish to rely on that happening.

Self-discipline and focus is a habit. It is like being competitive. Athletes are competitive at everything, whether it is their own sport, throwing snowballs or playing cards. The same goes for self-discipline and focus. You are what you habitually do, so form the right habits. Habits can be formed and broken. Although there is a perceived wisdom that it takes between 21 and 28 days to break a habit, it is actually very variable depending on who you are and what habit you are trying to break. I always liked the image of watching your fingernails grow. If you keep watching them you will see nothing but after a while you will be able to look and see that they have grown. Patience and persistence is the key. Get organised, plan ahead, tidy desk, tidy mind, be prepared, be here now, and focus on one thing at a time. Whatever cue you need to get your habits sorted, live by it.

Media Skill

Look at every single aspect of your life as an opportunity to improve your marketability. I know of a local school that does a public speaking course alongside A-levels. If you have that kind of opportunity, then take it, because public speaking is definitely a skill that will help you earn a living in sport. Drama or acting can give you similar skills. These might be the last thing you would think of as a help, but remember that in most sports, you do not make a lot of money from the sport itself. Therefore, although you want to pursue your sport, you need to understand how you earn a living from your sport as well and understand what skills you need to do that.

Think about the number of sportsmen and women you see on TV shows such as Sky's League of Their Own, BBC's Question of Sport, and Top Gear, and as commentators on sports programmes. To be able to do this, they have to have media skills. Just like everything else you do, to become skilled at this takes practice. You are not going to get opportunities for this kind of thing if you are mumbling and monosyllabic.

Networking

To get opportunities, originally starting with sponsors, you need to push yourself forward and be cheeky. No-one is going to pop up and suddenly decide to give you money so there is very little success to be gained from "cold-calling". You have to develop relationships. It isn't cynical to think that every single person you meet may be a potential sponsor or be able to hook you up with a sponsor. In business this is called networking and not only is it acceptable, it is expected. Businesses are a two-way street and creating a network is mutually beneficial for all parties. The key to successfully networking is to ensure you have something to offer as well as something you need. You must look for mutually beneficial relationships with people. Sometimes you will be the beneficiary and sometimes you will be the benefactor, but you must be prepared to accept both and only expect to come out even in the long term. Plant your acorns and see where they grow.

Sponsorship

There are different types of sponsor. There are the ones that will support you with their own products like energy drinks, supplements or equipment. On the one hand these may be easier because they tend to have big budgets and in the early days you will be looking for very little, but getting your shoes supplied for free might be a big help. On the other hand, there will probably be a lot of people looking to get in with these companies. This is why a relationship helps.

The other type of sponsor is a company who have no direct link with sport but will support you in some aspect of your journey. Just asking someone like this for money is very unlikely to be successful, even if you already have a relationship with them. They are not charities. They will not give you money so you can afford to buy your next PlayStation game. What they might do is to support a particular aspect of your training. It might be that they would pay for your Gym membership, or for physiotherapy, or your hotel or travel costs. But remember, just calling someone up out of the blue is not going to get you a fat cheque. You need to rely on the people you know, or companies that you have a connection with via friends or family. So it stands to reason that the more people you know, the more opportunity you have. Also, remember that asking for support is less likely to be successful if you cannot offer something in return.

Give and Take

As an athlete, you have a lot to give, although you might not know it. Depending on your age, you can build on the skills and knowledge you pick up along the way and can then use those skills and knowledge to offer something back to your sponsors. Later on in your career speaking to corporate teams is very lucrative, so getting to see sportsmen doing this if you ever have an opportunity is worth spending some time on. But you also know a lot about sport and fitness. Could you train to become a coach yourself? Coaching at little Johnny's school in return for his father's company supporting you financially would be one example. Could your skills be transferred to fitness training for the employees?

Some companies will support you as an employee. If you are already a high performer, they can employ you as an ambassador and you work for them to suit your training. Although these situations are rare, they do exist, and it is something the armed forces are particularly good at.

Brand You

The financial side of sport is similar to any business. Essentially, you are a salesman selling "brand you". If you want people to buy your product you have to sell it to them. It has to be a slow process and you are best starting early. Sow many seeds; build up many relationships. Build your brand. Be aware of how people will get information about you. If you have a Facebook and Twitter page then be aware of what is on it. Being tagged at parties, drinking alcohol and looking worse for wear isn't really going to help. If you think you will not be researched, think again. However, you are probably young; you have more social media skills than most older people. Use this to your advantage, advertise yourself. Use your Facebook page to post about your training. Link it in with a YouTube account showing your performances. Post pictures on your twitter account of you winning medals. Used LinkedIn as well, it is surprising how that can work for you and the number of helpful professionals on there. Use your skills, promote yourself. If you have opinions you would like to post then do so, but make sure they are the kind of things that you want people to read about. Avoid abusive conversations that are on the record in the public domain. If you want to have fun with your peers and friends, do it by private message so it does not show up in your timeline. Use your public profile for what you want people to know about you, for managing your brand.

The other thing you can do is to create a blog. Publish your training and your competition comments. People will be able to see how you are performing, how you have progressed and how hard you are training. I have mentioned it before but take a look at Giavanni Ruffin's YouTube videos and Mike Sweeney's "A day in the life of…". These two have both used YouTube to publicise themselves and get sponsorship or opportunities.

Summary

In all, if you reach the top, the elite level in your sport, then all types of people will be interested in you. If nothing else, following the advice in this chapter will get you used to meeting and talking to lots of people in a variety of different mediums. At best it could get you the support or sponsorship you need to get to the top. Either way, like the rest of this book, you have nothing to lose and everything to gain.

1. Create 'Brand You' and be the brand.

2. Actively network with people.

3. Be cheeky, do not be shy about talking about needing support, but do not just outright ask for sponsorship in the very first conversation with someone. Build a relationship.

4. Develop skills you might need, take opportunities to learn.

5. Use your social networking skills for positive networking and promotion.

6. Create a blog or other promotional site.

CHAPTER 5

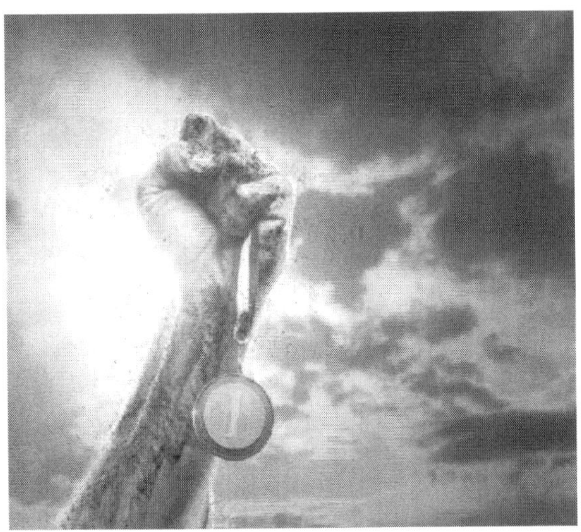

MOTIVATION

Motivation –

noun

a reason or reasons for acting or behaving in a particular way:

desire or willingness to do something; enthusiasm:

"motivation". Oxford Dictionaries. April 2010. Oxford Dictionaries. April 2010. Oxford University Press. 08 January 2013

<http://oxforddictionaries.com/definition/english/motivation>.

Motivation is everything. What is your motivation for training, for competing? What is your reason for performing, for striving for the success of your dream? To quote Eric Thomas, "What's your why?"

"A hungry for success athlete is a dangerous athlete, I'm not hungry, I'm absolutely starving!!" – Andy Turner (1980-) European and Commonwealth Games Gold medal-winning 110m Hurdler

What's your why?

If you are young, you probably have not given a great deal of thought to your motivation, as it might be that the love of the game is enough. You are doing something you enjoy and it is only now, when you have been recognised as having 'talent' that you are starting to take things a bit more seriously. In previous chapters, I have already covered that your dream has to be big enough to get you through the pain and sacrifice; that the common factor with elite performers is their desire. But now it is time to consider where that desire comes from and what sustains it.

Knowing something and acting on that knowledge are two very different things. Knowing that smoking is very bad for you and not smoking are entirely different. Everyone knows that smoking is bad for you, but a lot of people smoke, including doctors. The knowing and the doing are very different. Two equally 'talented' athletes may know that getting up an hour earlier to do an extra session for the day will benefit them but that does not mean that they will both do it. The difference between the two is in their desire, their motivation.

"The ones who want to achieve and win championships motivate themselves." –Mike Ditka (1939-) American Football Player, Coach and TV Commentator

Burning Desire

There are hundreds of books and theories on motivation, but for your purpose, it is about what drives you. What gets you through the things that you have to get through? I have seen young sprinters doing a lactic tolerance session who have vomited between repetitions, or been in so much pain from the lactic build up in their legs that they have crawled back to their starting position to be ready for the next one and still dragged themselves upright and started on the whistle. What drives them? It isn't me as coach. I don't shout at them. I have a simple rule – "The gate's not locked". This means that you do it or don't do it. I can't do it for you, you are only here because you want to be and I'm not forcing you to do anything. What drives them? Whatever it is, each of them will be different and that will be different for you. What drives you to spend less time with your friends, to go through pain, to leave your PlayStation switched off? What drives you to skip that party, to train on your birthday, on Christmas day?

"One important aspect of character is a ceaseless desire to improve." - John Wooden, legendary US College Football Coach, won an unprecedented 10 NCAA Championships in 12 years (1910-2010)

Your dream is about what you are aiming for, what you are trying to achieve, but your motivation is about why you are doing it. It might be that you are trying to get somewhere for yourself or for your family. You might be trying to get away from somewhere, your surroundings or your circumstances. It might be as simple as that you are driven to win a gold medal in the Olympics for the pride. Maybe you have a family member, dead or alive, that means a lot to you that you are doing this for.

"The more reasons you have for achieving your goal, the more determined you will become." - Brian Tracy (1944-) Motivational Speaker and Author

Achieving sporting success defies many of the normal theories of motivation. One of the most basic and often quoted motivation theories is Maslow's Hierarchy of

Needs, which states that motivation can be categorized into five needs which work in levels. In simple terms you must fulfil the lower level needs before the higher level needs become motivators. In order, from the lowest level needs, these are Physiological (breathing, food, water etc), Safety (security, health, freedom from pain), love/belonging (friendship, family, and relationships), Esteem (confidence, achievement, respect) and self-actualization ("to become everything one is capable of becoming"). So the theory goes that your safety would take priority over your need to be respected, which makes perfect sense.

However, in athletes, the theory in its simplest form starts to break down. The highest level need is so strong that it becomes stronger than the lower level needs. An athlete will give up friendship, relationships, put himself or herself through pain, put themselves in real danger to achieve success. Their motivation to achieve is so strong, it overrides their safety and security need.

Eric Thomas the motivational speaker who works with a lot of US sports teams in Baseball, NFL and Basketball, describes this in one of his talks on motivation.

There was a young man, who wanted to make a lot of money and so, he went to this guru. He told the guru "I wanna be at the same level as you are". And so the guru said, "If you want to be at the same level I'm on, I'll meet you tomorrow at the beach".

So the young man got there at 4am, he's all ready to rock and roll, got on a suit (he should've wore shorts). The old man grabbed his hands and said "How bad do you want to be successful?". He said "Real bad".

The guru said "Walk on out into the water". So he walks out into the water, and when he walks out into the water, it goes waist deep. And he was like "This guy's crazy" and went "Hey, I want you to teach me how to make money, but you are teaching me how to swim. I didn't ask to be a lifeguard. I want to make money!".

He went "Come out a little further" and the young man walked out a little further where the water is deeper. And he was like "This old man is crazy…he makin' money but he crazy". The old man said "Come out a little further" and he went a little further. The water was right at his mouth…The young man went "I don't want to proceed anymore" and the old man said "I thought you want to be successful!". And the young man said "I do!". And the old man went "Then, walk a little further". The young man did, then he dropped his head in the water and the old man held him down, he had him held down, just when the young man was about to pass out, he raised him up.

He said, "When you were under water what did you want to do?"

Young man said, "I wanted to breathe."

He told the guy "When you want to succeed as bad as you want to breathe, then you will be successful".

If you ever had an asthma attack before, you're short of breath, you're wheezing. The only thing you are trying to do, is get some air. You don't care about no basketball game, you don't care what's on the TV, you don't care about the parties… The only thing you care about when you are trying to breathe, is to get some fresh air. That's it. And when you get to the point when all you want to do is to be successful as bad as you want to breathe, then you will be successful.

Take this example from a Sports Illustrated article in 1990; a scenario, from a 1995 poll of 198 sprinters, swimmers, powerlifters and other assorted athletes, most of them US Olympians or aspiring Olympians.

You are offered a banned performance-enhancing substance that comes with two guarantees:

1) You will not be caught.

2) You will win every competition you enter for the next five years, and then you will die from the side effects of the substance. Would you take it?

More than half the athletes said yes.

It may be that answering something intellectually and actually doing it are different things. With the onset of retrospective testing and bans, the answers may be different now, but the mindset that would allow half the athletes to answer yes to that question with its consequences shows how far many are prepared to go.

The Five Why's

Ask yourself why you want to achieve the level of success you have dreamed of. What drives you? In some cases, especially at a young age, it might be money or fast cars or a big house. It might be adulation of people around you, maybe even celebrity status.

This will not get you to where you want to be. The person who has a more deep and meaningful motivation than money or fame will be capable of greater things than you. Money and fame are a consequence of your sporting success. (In some cases, though, even success at the highest level does not bring money and fame.) If you chase money and celebrity, what happens if you get them before you become successful?

"People often say that motivation doesn't last. Well, neither does bathing - that's why we recommend it daily." - Zig Ziglar (1926-2012) Author and Motivational Speaker

This could explain why track and field in the UK is relatively unsuccessful. Once athletes achieve the podium level of funding, they have 'made it'. They become funded and have achieved their goals before they have achieved success. They get all the advantages of extra coaches, training camps, massage, nutrition but it does not make them better because they settle, they become satisfied. They aren't hungry any more.

Many believe that the same thing happened to British Swimming in the aftermath of the Beijing Olympics. Funding is allocated based on success. Swimming was successful and over-achieved in terms of medals and so more funding came through. What happened? Under-achievement in the London Olympics and loss of funding.

"If you want to be number one, you have to train like you're number two" – Maurice Green (1979-) Former 100m Sprinter and World Record Holder

Ask yourself 'Why' you want to be successful. When you have your answer ask why for that answer and keep asking why until you go no further. This usually takes five 'Why's', hence the name. This was developed by Sakichi Toyoda for Toyota Motor Corporation as a problem solving tool to get to the root cause of any problem, but it is worth trying to understand why you want to get to your goal.

You have to be hungry for success. Hungry to the extent that (metaphorically) eating does not satisfy you, it makes you hungrier. Being the best in your District makes you hungry to be the best in your County. Best in your County makes you hungry to be best in your Area. Then Country, then Continent, and then the World. If you are the best in the World, you should want to be the best there has ever been and the best there ever will be. Your desire should have no end, otherwise when you get there, what will you do?

Intrinsic Motivation

"It's not the push from behind or the pull from the front - it's the drive from inside." - Dale Brown, US College Basketball Coach (1935-present)

Your motivation must come from deep inside you. It should be intrinsic. It should not need a coach or a competitor to motivate you. Dr Chris Stankovich of Advanced Human Performance Systems has worked with many US Football and Major League Baseball players and states that "since intrinsic motivation is based on a person's individual values it is nearly impossible for others (parents and coaches) to instil these values in people." They may be a vehicle to help you but they are extrinsic motivators, not the source of your motivation. Parents should not be living their life through you nor should you be trying to achieve something to please them, as that will not last. This is about your own desire.

The Australian Commission for Sport found that elite athletes are driven by self-determination reasons and actively seek autonomy. In sport particularly, most are motivated by being the best they can possibly be. This is a positive cycle because there is always more that you can be; you can always get better. Your body will always surprise you. When you hit what you think is your maximum you will find that actually there is more, that your maximum has become your comfortable. You will step it up, again and again, constantly pushing your own boundaries, testing the limits of performance. Although “being the best you can be” may seem a little bland as a motivation, it is the most powerful of all and is the one thing that in my research that determines how successful you will be.

“The principle is competing against yourself. It's about self improvement, about being better than you were the day before.” – Steve Young (1961-) Former American Football player.

Your desire is driven by how strongly you feel about achieving your dream. When you think about it, it should hurt. It should hurt that you are not there yet, you should be jealous of the people that are.

"Winning isn't everything, but wanting to is." – Vince Lombardi (1930-1979) American Football Player and Coach

As Liz Yelling the double Olympian marathon runner, told the Guardian in an interview in 2009, “Novice or Olympian, we all struggle with motivation sometimes. On dark, wet nights, when I do not feel like a run, I remind myself that my competitors will be out there doing their runs. I want that edge over them, and that's all the motivation I need."

"You and your opponent want the same thing. The only thing that matters is who works the hardest for it." – Unknown

Will Smith is an actor, producer, and rapper but sums up what real motivation and desire means in an interview with Travis Smiley.

"The only thing that I see that is distinctly different about me is I'm not afraid to die on a treadmill. I will not be outworked, period.

"You might have more talent than me, you might be smarter than me, or you might be sexier than me. You might be all of those things and you got it on me in nine categories. But if we get on a treadmill together, there's two things. Either you get off first, or I'm going to die. It's really that simple.

You're not going to outwork me."

Summary

Get under your own skin. You can be honest with yourself; you do not have to tell everyone what your inner desire is. If you really want to stand at the top of that podium in the Olympics, or taking that shot on the 18th green for the Ryder Cup, or the last penalty in the World Cup and if you want it enough that you would do anything to get there, then that is your why.

There is only one action from this chapter, a question to answer:

1. What's your why?

CHAPTER 6

SACRIFICE

"Understand that there is a price to be paid for anything of significance. You must be willing to pay that price." - John Wooden, legendary US College Football Coach, won an unprecedented 10 NCAA Championships in 12 years (1910-2010)

You cannot have everything. It is a simple fact of life that if you prioritise one thing it means something else has to make way. This is the case for everything in life, it is the reality. If you meet a partner and share their life, then you will have to give something up to make room for them. If you have kids, then there are definitely things that need to go. Athletes that get to an elite level know they have made sacrifices to do so. The important thing is that they also know that they have traded off something of lesser importance for something of great importance. This is the key to sacrifice.

How to give things up.

"A man can be as great as he wants to be. If you believe in yourself and have the courage, the determination, the dedication, the competitive drive and if you are willing to sacrifice the little things in life and pay the price for the things that are worthwhile, it can be done." – Vince Lombardi (1930-1979) American Football Player and Coach

If what you have to sacrifice is unpalatable to achieve your dream, then you will not be able to do it. The choice, once it's time to make it, should be easy. You do not need to hide from it or dress it up as something else. You need to make the decision. If you decide that you are not ready to make a particular sacrifice, then so be it, just make the decision consciously. Stand up to it. Do not kid yourself. At least this way, you can rationally revisit the decision you made if the circumstances change. You might find your improvement stalls at some point and you need to take the next step. Something that was important to you before may not be as important to you now. Or it might not have made much of a difference when you decided, but now it will. If you hide from these decisions then you will not be able to review them.

Choosing not to make a sacrifice at any given time does not make you a bad person or a bad athlete no matter what anyone tells you. You are the only one walking (running or playing) in your shoes and only you can decide what is right.

"Opportunity may knock only once, but temptation leans on the doorbell" - Unknown

The Expendables

Now that we have covered how not to make a sacrifice, it's time to look at what you may need to sacrifice to achieve your goal and your dream, what is expendable. The most obvious thing that you will sacrifice is time. While you are doing all the things you need to do, training, competing, recovering and everything that goes with them, then you are not doing something else. Sport is a huge commitment and often outside of work, school or sleep, it is the biggest time expenditure in your life.

"The speed of your success is limited only by your dedication and what you;re willing to sacrifice." - Nathan W Morriss, Author (present)

It does not matter who you are or how good you are, the amount of time you have available is the same for everyone, 24 hours, 1,440 minutes, or 86,400 seconds, so use them wisely. It is important to manage your time effectively, but that is not difficult. Most people do not realise how much time they are wasting. A simple way to manage your time is to start with a piece of paper broken down into 24 hours. You can draw the shape of a clock face or just 24, one hour time slots (or better still 48, ½ hour slots) as shown in the diagram. Now colour in the times you are asleep (not what time you go to bed if this includes still watching TV or texting, but what time you settle down to sleep), the times you are at school or work, the times you are at training and the other mandatory times such as revision or homework. If you have other things you know that take your time up then add them in, such as eating, hygiene and the like, but be honest about how long these take, do not put an hour in if they only take half an hour.

What you have left is all your free time for texting, talking to friends, games and downtime. Do this for the whole week. Pay particular attention to the weekend as this is when your time is usually used up on other things that aren't mandatory. If you need to add something like more training to get better, then where does this fit? If it does not fit in as it stands, or you aren't prepared to give up your other activities, it's time to have a look at that big block of time called sleep.

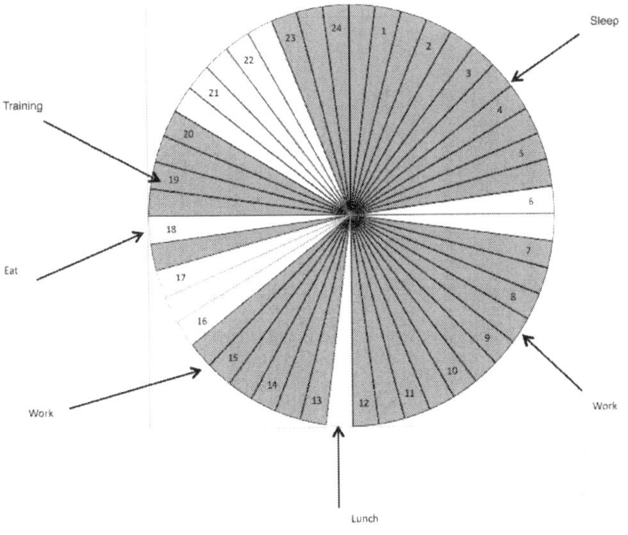

The Big Sleep

Now that sleep has been mentioned, this is likely to be another sacrifice that you have to make. While it is nice to have lie-ins on the weekend, you will probably be up early to train or compete. You might need to get up early all week to get an early training session in before school or work in addition to the evening one. Obviously, you need to get enough sleep, but there is a difference between "enough" and "a nice relaxing lie-in".

I'm not about to tell you how much sleep is enough for you, you can work that out for yourself, but don't kid yourself. I am sure if you try hard enough you can convince yourself that you cannot cut back on your sleep, because you need it for recovery. The second part is true, but the first part probably isn't. Even if it is, go to bed earlier as a late night after training isn't beneficial, but an early morning so you can get an extra session in is.

Collateral Damage

Friends and the things that go with them also suffer. Because you are so focussed on your sport and have less time than most, your friends that are outside your sport circle will be unlikely to understand. They will not be as close as they might be. They might resent not having your time when they need it or want it. You cannot attend parties or other social events due to training and competition. You will not get involved in some of the things that they might, things like drinking and smoking or experimenting with recreational drugs, which will set you apart from the group. You will have an 'athlete-switch' that will kick in to remind you of the consequences of what you are doing that your friends just do not have (you may not realise it but this is similar to the 'parent-switch' which takes the edge off going out for a late night and drinking too much when you know your infant is going to be awake and loud in a few hours!). You have more reasons for not drinking than for drinking; training the next day, the effect on your body, ability to recover from training.

Then there are the little things that may need to be sacrificed. Time on the Playstation or the X-Box. Time on Facebook, Twitter or other social media. Mobile phone use, certain foods and drinks. Being a serious athlete is pervasive. It affects everything you do. These are the sacrifices elite athletes make to achieve what they want to achieve. It's not just sport that requires a sacrifice like this. Anything that needs a high level of commitment requires similar sacrifice; becoming a parent, being an A-student, a career.

"Everybody can get excited to play in the games. But are you willing to pay the price and sacrifice in the off-season?" - Peyton Manning, US Football Quarterback and holds the record for most career touchdown passes (1976 - present)

There are those who would prefer you not to know what it takes to become elite because it might put you off. If knowing how difficult it will be would put you off, then it is unlikely that you will make it to the top anyway. I hope you'll have found that this book has not pulled any punches so far and this chapter is probably the one that punches hardest. But if you think you can take an easy route to the top then you will not make it. It does not mean you have to become a monk and only work, train and sleep at the expense of everything else. You just need to make choices and make them consciously.

Decision Time

So how do you decide? In the first instance, your choices should be around doing what you need to do for the level you are at. In your early development, you will probably be doing a lot of sport because you love it, your friends will all be playing or participating, the amount and type of training will be varied. You probably will not feel you are making any sacrifices particularly because you do not know any different, you are just doing what you love doing. As you get older, into your mid to late teens, other things will start to come into play such as girlfriends or boyfriends and the more active social lives of the group around you. As kids get older, they get more freedom, but freedom for you may just mean you can travel to training on your own instead of a parent taking you, whereas your friends are going into town or doing stuff with their other friends.

This is where the work you did in Chapter 1 becomes important. Revisit your dream. Do you still want it? Is it still a burning desire that means the sacrifices you are making are all worth it to achieve what you want it to be? If you feel very matter-of-fact about your sacrifices, in other words you know you are making them but they do not seem all that big, then you are in the right place. If you feel a real sense of loss, of missing out, then you need to re-evaluate your balance. Take care, though, as sometimes you will get a temporary sense of it all not being worth it. There are times in any sport, such as when you are in the depths of winter training far from competition season, where you will just be grinding it out. You know what these points are, you know how they feel. You just have to get through the grind because you know it will be worth it in the summer (or vice versa). These are not the times to re-evaluate anything. If you are going to re-evaluate, do it in the middle of your season when you know you can take a reasonable judgement.

When it comes to making decisions over sacrifices, approach it with a positive frame of mind. Do I want “x” more than I want to achieve my dream. A wise man once said, “There is nothing more dangerous nor misleading than the right answer to the wrong question”. So frame your questions to yourself carefully. As renowned motivational speaker and author Eric Thomas puts it, do not ask what’s wrong with something; ask what is right with it. That is the right question. “What’s wrong with skipping training once in a while” becomes “What’s right with skipping training once in a while” and so on.

It is worth repeating that this does not mean you have to be a monk. If you are given the opportunity to go to watch a big game and it clashes with training, you can still answer “what’s right with that”. You need to keep your dream alive and doing things like that are important. You might even be able to make up the training time elsewhere in the day or week.

“If you are going to be a champion, you must be willing to pay a greater price.” – Bud Wilkinson (1916-1994) US NFL Footballer, coach, broadcaster and politician

Eli Goldratt, writer of "The Goal", whom you will hear more of in Chapter 13, has a technique called Evaporating the Cloud. The principle of Evaporating the Cloud is that any dilemma can be boiled down to the choice between two conflicting options (or actions), and that there are a series of assumptions holding this conflict in place. Rather than keep swinging between the two options with the obvious compromise to the other, Goldratt suggests that it is the assumptions that should be challenged so that the needs served by both actions can be met. This sounds a bit complicated until you see it in an example.

Take a simple conflict. On the one hand, I want to train, on the other hand I want to go out with my mates, which stops me training (it helps if the choices are framed in direct opposition to other). We now need to understand what need is being fulfilled by each of the two options (or courses of action). So, I want to train so that I will improve. I want to go out with my mates so that I keep an active social life beyond sport. Both of these are necessary to be a fulfilled and motivated person. Once we put the assumptions in place now, the picture becomes a little clearer.

I cannot train and go out with my mates *because both of these are at the same time.*

I want to train so that I will improve *because I am working to a training schedule that is important.*

I want to go out with my mates so that I keep an active social life beyond sport *because going out with my mates at this particular time is important to me.*

I need both sport and social life to be a fulfilled and motivated *person because neither is sufficient on its own to maintain my level of commitment to my dream.*

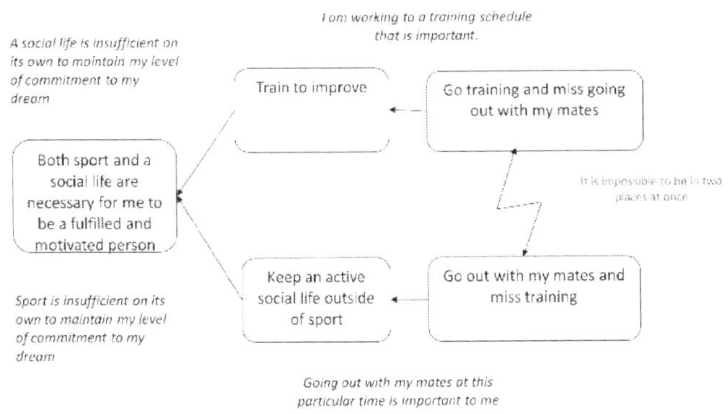

The assumptions that are holding this dilemma, or conflict, in place are the statements after the word 'because' or outside the boxes on the perimeter of the diagram. If you look at each of these in turn, they can be challenged to see whether the cloud hanging over you evaporates. In the first statement, is it necessary that both are at the same time? In a team sport, it might not be possible to miss a team training session, but in an individual sport you might be able to train earlier or later in the day, in which case the conflict goes away. Are your mates doing something specific that can only be done at that time or is there another time you can join them?

In the second statement your training schedule is important but how does this particular session fall within it? Is there something else you can do to achieve the same result? Maybe even a better result.

In the third statement, is the only way to maintain your social life going out with these mates at this time? Would your mates rearrange for you? If you wanted to go a bit deeper, if your social circle was made up of your team mates then everyone's social life would be on the same time plan.

The last one is probably unbreakable; you need both statements to maintain your balance as a person. You need downtime and social interaction.

Overall you should be able to see that looking at the assumptions as to why you have a conflict and breaking these to evaporate the cloud is the least destructive of the options you have. If you choose one over the other, then you will be conflicted because you will lose out on one. If you compromise, then you will do a bit of both and inevitably lose out a bit on both. Evaporating the cloud is about having the best of both worlds. It will not always work, but it is certainly worth considering before the sacrifice needs to be made.

A new perspective on Sacrifice

To achieve the next level of athletic performance requires a greater sacrifice than to maintain the one that you currently perform at. Such sacrifice requires a new level of mental toughness and a new mindset, a new approach to the sacrifices.

I have seen the writing of many people about the nature of sacrifice in respect to athletes pursuing their dreams of greatness. On the one hand, there are arguments that there must be sacrifices made to achieve an elite level and that no-one can attain that without making many of them along the way. On the other hand, there are those who believe that the pursuit of sporting glory holds such reward that there should be no feeling of sacrifice or of giving things up to achieve it, that if there is a feeling of sacrifice then the desire isn't great enough and the pursuit will be unsustainable and short-lived.

Both of those standpoints are incorrect as they are merely short term views of the journey to becoming an elite athlete. Taking a longer view is not only more motivational for you as an athlete but also lessens the issue significantly. This change comes in two parts - a change of timescale and the change of perspective.

Firstly, sacrifice is about giving something up. Making a sacrifice in a sporting context in pursuit of a goal involves making a choice of "what you want to do versus what you must do". In all sporting biographies there are anecdotes of the choices made; birthday parties missed, holidays, family gatherings and so on. The list is endless, but the nature of the sacrifice is in the description of the choices made at the time.

Pursuing an elite level in sport requires not sacrifice as such, but postponement. If the previous statement is re-written as "making a choice of what you want to do today, versus what you must do today" then the context is more relevant to your journey, less divisive and more palatable. These choices have to be made and they will still be difficult, especially for young athletes in the early stages of their career, and no doubt they will still be seen as sacrifices at the time. However, by seeing the decision as postponing one choice in deference to the other they can be taken more easily.

There are many things that must be delayed to assume the mantle of an elite athlete, but usually the career of an athlete is relatively short-lived and the rewards are great (although not necessarily financial). At an extreme, delaying choices like marriage, children, holidays and so on until you are 30 may seem like a long way off to a young athlete, but all these opportunities will still be available then.

"I hated every minute of training, but I said, 'Don't quit. Suffer now and live the rest of your life as a champion'." — Muhammad Ali (1942-) Former professional boxer and considered by many to be the greatest heavyweight of all time.

In a smaller sense, delaying the partying, the socialising, and birthday celebrations to the off-season breaks is possible in most sports and makes these things seem less far away. In many ways, depressurising after a long season can be beneficial.

Many successful business people, women especially, will put off having a family until they have achieved their career goals. It is rarely seen as a permanent decision, and athletes should adopt the same approach instead of seeing these things as a choice between one and the other. As a friend in manufacturing used to say "You can have everything, you just can't have it all at once".

The second part of the change in mindset about sacrifice is that a change of perspective is needed. Sacrifice is seen more often than not only through the eyes of the athlete, looking at what they have had to give up. But life is generally fair. You can't have everything at once. If you chase two rabbits you will catch neither. It wouldn't be a fair world if you could go out partying with your friends, drinking, smoking, and staying out late and yet still be an elite athlete. That would be greedy. Change your perspective and view the sacrifice from the other side, from 'their' side. It isn't about your sacrifice, it is about their compensation. You get to compete in front of a packed 100,000 crowd. Their compensation is that they get to do the things you do not. It is a natural balance. While you do not get to do all the things you want to when you want to do them, they do not get to compete at the highest level with whatever rewards that entails. It is only fair that the others get compensated in life and an athlete should not begrudge them that compensation or expect to be able to share it.

Is that all?

Often, though, a sacrifice does have to be made so, in the end, think on it like this. Project yourself forward and picture yourself being interviewed on TV ahead of the Olympic Games, the World Cup, the World Championships or whatever your dream entails, and imagine you are asked the question by a presenter "What did you have to give up to get where you are today?".

Now think of the decision you are making, the sacrifice you think you are making and imagine yourself answering the interviewer. See if it sounds right.

"Well, Claire (Balding), I could only play on my Playstation for 2 hours a day on the weekends when my mates were on it longer. It meant they got to Prestige on Black Ops 3 quicker than I did."

"It was hard, Gary (Lineker), when my mates were hanging out in the park drinking Cider; I was out playing football in the field."

"I had to get up 30 minutes earlier every day, Sue (Barker) to do my core exercises so I could fit them in."

Is that it? Was that all it took? Obviously a lot of these decisions are small, and added up they may be the straw that breaks the camels back, but it certainly puts your dilemma into context.

If you need further context, look around at what others give up to achieve their dreams. Some sports are a lot harder than others. Swimmers train early and late most days. The early is very early, usually 5am. There are two reasons for this. The first is so that sufficient recovery is possible before the next training session in the evening. The second is that is when the pool is available! How many swimmers do you think are still hitting Facebook and Skype at midnight if they have to be at the pool by 5am? Gymnasts, also, train hard and often, their conditioning work is legendary and their flexibility work is brutal. Then there are the triathletes who are training for three endurance events. These guys also train twice a day to fit everything in. Theirs is not just a sacrifice; their whole life revolves around training. Every athlete believes their life revolves around their sport, but if you meet a triathlete, talk to them about their training and lifestyle and you will see what I mean. Finally, there are the multi-event athletes who do decathlon and heptathlon who are a completely different breed to us mere mortals. If training for one event is not hard enough, training for ten is beyond most people's comprehension. Mike Sweeney, the up and coming British decathlete, has made a video on YouTube called 'A week in the life of……'.

While the sacrifices you make may seem quite difficult at the time, when you look back on it afterwards, they will not seem like a sacrifice at all. You need to look at it through a wider-angle lens.

Summary

Finally, look at your parents and what they sacrifice for you. The time they put in, the money they spend. It is not really a sacrifice to them because they want to do these things for you. They put their lives on hold to ferry you around. They put their own ambitions on hold, sporting or otherwise, to give you the opportunities. That is not to say that you aren't grateful, it is only to point out that the sacrifices that you think you are making are probably not that big. Once you recognise that, they don't seem that important when weighed against what you can achieve, although they may seem big at the time.

1. Create 7 time clock faces in ½ hour intervals, one for each day of the week.

2. Fill in your sleep, work/school and training times.

3. Identify your leisure time and what you do in it.

4. If you have a conflict or dilemma write it out as described, including all the 'Because' statements

5. Review the 'Because' statements to see if you can evaporate the cloud and fulfil both needs.

6. Adjust your perspective

7. Adjust your timeframe

This will allow you to be tough enough to make the necessary sacrifices that are inevitable.

Part 2 – Putting it into Practice

Chapter 7

Getting Started

The key to getting started is to get started! Newton's First Law of Motion states that a body at rest will stay at rest until a **Force** is exerted on it. You are that force.

On Your Marks, Get Set, GO!

Do not be overwhelmed by the size of the task. You have a big dream, but you are not going to achieve that tomorrow, otherwise it is not very big at all. (If you are in the Olympic final tomorrow, I take that back!). You will have your waypoints, but even those will seem to be a long way away. Even the waypoints will probably be challenging and, at the point where you haven't started your journey, they may seem a little overwhelming in themselves. However, do not worry, as Laozi, Founder of the Taoist philosophy says "A journey of a thousand miles must begin with a single step." So start from where you are and what you have, moving towards your goal. This is far more positive than starting from where you want to be and what you want to have then fretting over the gap.

"Chance favours those in motion." - James Austin (1925-) US Neurologist and author

The Duvet Moment

Once you know you are heading in the right direction, get moving. Keep moving in that direction and make your course adjustments on the way. While I was training as a coach, the tutor called this the 'Duvet' moment. He explained he usually rode his bike early in the morning to miss the heavy traffic and his regular challenge was to ride to the top of a hill many miles away. To get to the top of the hill, he knew he had a few mini-waypoints. A post-box two-thirds of the way up, a shop half way up and so on. To get to the top, he had to pass through those waypoints but first he had to get to the bottom and that meant riding for a couple of hours. He was only going to do that if he got on his bike and started riding. To get on his bike he needed to be in his kit and outside. To get in his kit, he had to be out of bed and getting out of bed started when his alarm clock went off, and he threw back his duvet. As soon as he did that he knew he would get to the top of the hill a few hours later. If he did anything else, started to negotiate with himself, put the alarm clock on snooze, or rolled over and switched it off, he would not make it to the top of the hill. Everything started with the first single act of throwing off the duvet as soon as the alarm went off - The 'Duvet' moment. You may not know the whole route to the top of your first hill, but you do know that if you do not take that first step, you won't be able to take you 21st or your 101st and so on.

"If we wait for the moment when everything, absolutely everything, is ready, we shall never begin" – Ivan Turgenev (1818-1883) Russian author and playwright

The next thing then is not to take too much on yourself. You have done the hard work now. Take one day at a time, one training session at a time or even one rep at a time. Once you are in motion you have started putting time in the bank and you'll be able to withdraw it in competition at a later date.

"Have a bias towards action. You can break that big plan into small steps and take that first step straight away" – Indira Gandhi (1917-1984) Longest serving and first female prime minister of India

You may well have been playing a sport for a long time as a child, and you might have been practising regularly. But until you have really locked in on your destination, your journey hasn't really started. Once it has, once you have taken that first step, then the planning stage is over. You have done your research; you have recognised what it is that you need to do to become elite. You have made your plans. Now it is time to prepare yourself for everything that comes next. Prepare your body and your mind for each step, each game, and each competition.

"Nobody can go back and start a new beginning, but anyone can start today and make a new ending" – Maria Robinson (present) Scottish doctor and author

"Don't do, Pursue".

From now on you are no longer just doing a sport. You are now pursuing your dream. Others around you may be dreaming and hoping, but you are in a place that is more than hope. Your motivation is higher, you have a burning desire to get to your dream and you are now pursuing it. Every game you play, every training session you attend, every practice you do on your own is working towards that goal. It is the difference between putting in effort in a training session because your coach is shouting at you, to putting everything in because this is another step towards the dream you are pursuing. Every step, every set, every rep moves you closer to achieving your dream.

"There are only two options regarding commitment; you're either in or you're out. There's no

such thing as life in-between." – Pat Riley (1945-) US NBA Basketball former player and coach, now executive.

While you are pursuing that dream, you have to make sure that you improve every single time you step on that pitch, on that track, or on that court. It may be raining, cold, snowing, hot, humid, or some other kind of miserable weather. Everyone else just wants to get through the game and get home, but this is another opportunity to improve. You never know when the scouts are there. It might be your opportunity to play for the district, the county, or the national team. These are the days when it matters most, when other people do not want it as badly as you do, because they are just 'doing' whereas you are 'pursuing'.

Summary

Part 2 of this book is about how to make your practice purposeful. How to make sure that you are improving and challenging yourself to achieve what you want to achieve now that you have got started.

1. Throw off the duvet.
2. Stop planning and start moving.
3. Don't 'do', pursue.

CHAPTER 8

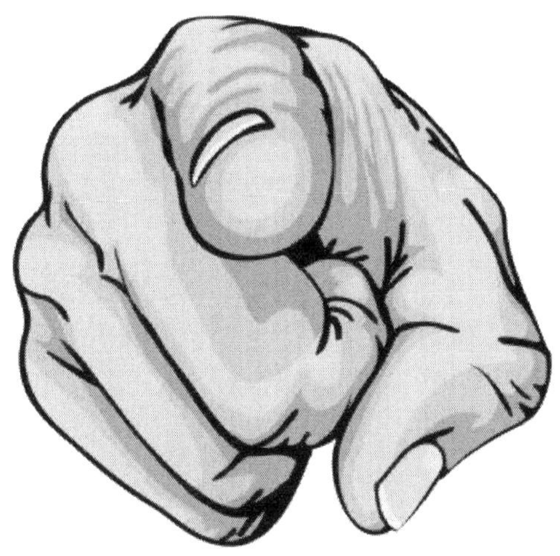

IT'S ALL ABOUT YOU

"If you blame others for something that happens in your life, then you must wait until they change in order to get better." – Wayne Dyer (1940-) US Self help author and motivational speaker

Once you make it, the glory is yours. You are the one who stands on the podium, or lifts the trophy, enjoys the success. So whose responsibility are all the activities that get you there? This may sound like a simple question and the answer is just as simple and obvious, but what does it really mean?

A simple way to understand what taking responsibility means is by using a few examples.

- You have a game, you are playing away, you are relying on one of your parents to pack your kit, but something has been forgotten.
- You were getting a lift with another teammate but they have misjudged the time so you have arrived late which means you do not have time to prepare.
- Your coach cannot make it and has not sent you the schedule.
- You are aiming for a big event, but you find out that your coach/parents/someone has forgotten to enter you or missed the deadline.

In all of these cases, someone else has let you down, so surely that was not your responsibility was it?

"Without proper self-evaluation, failure is inevitable." - John Wooden, legendary US College Football Coach, won an unprecedented 10 NCAA Championships in 12 years (1910-2010)

If you think like that, then you will consistently have examples like those I've listed. In some cases it might not matter. You can get over it or around it, but what if it happens at a very important time and affects your performance? You have to decide what you are prepared to risk. In business, relying on someone else to do something for you is known as delegation. You know generally who you can trust and with what, but one common rule is that, whilst you can delegate authority (in other words you can delegate or pass on the task to someone else), you cannot delegate the responsibility. So even if you are passing a task on to someone else, it is still your responsibility; if it goes wrong it's your fault. Once you understand this and take responsibility, it changes how you approach tasks and how you delegate them.

You can still delegate, you have to because you cannot do everything yourself, but you are more careful **how** you do it. So lets go back to the examples and break them down.

Kit

Relying on your parents to pack your kit because it has been in the laundry is reasonable to an extent. But if you know what you want packed, why not do the very final packing yourself. "Leave it on the bed Mum and I'll pack it". You now know it is there. If you are a bit disorganized, write a list and stick it on your wall. Then check you have everything before you leave. Simple. It prevents the problem and there's no drama.

Transport

If you are getting a lift, obviously the key point is that someone else is driving. That does not mean they know exactly what time **you** need to be there; they might not have the same schedule as you, or the same warm up routine. They might not be that good at judging journey times. Take the responsibility to find out what time you need to be setting off to arrive when **you** need to and ask to be picked up then. If your lift is a little more haphazard than you are, you might need to emphasize why you need to leave then, and how important it is. If they still are not accommodating, either find another lift or you have to accept the issue and work with it. Either way, you can adapt and be prepared.

Paperwork

The example described earlier in the chapter where your coach hasn't sent you the schedule is a classic. Your coach is human. They get sick, they get stuck in traffic, lose their phone or the phone runs out of power. Knowing your event schedule is a simple activity. Once you know what is happening and when, you can relax. The likelihood of your coach not being there for you is slim but you must be prepared regardless and if he is delayed for some reason then it doesn't affect your preparations.

Although your coach is doubtless a person that you admire and respect, they are human and by no means perfect. I have seen many coaches in many different sports who have been let down by their organizational skills. Being a coach requires being able to get the best out of athletes or teams. They have good people skills, they may be able to plan a whole season's training for a complex group of individuals but that does not automatically mean they are world class at administration. I have seen players who have got to the start of the season to find they have not been registered for the team, individual athletes who have mistakenly thought it is the coach who registers them with their sports governing body when it isn't and lost paperwork that has prevented some athletes from playing or competing.

You can take steps to lessen the impact of the problems, even though it is more difficult to be proactive in this case. First you need to find out what needs to be done. What do you need and when do you need it? What is the deadline, who does what? Do you need birth certificates, photos, parental consent forms, transfer forms? Just because you were registered last year does not mean you are registered this year. Missing a registration date or entry date catches out many people. Find out when you need to be registered by. If you need documents, get them in plenty of time. Make sure they are given to the right person. Keep copies in case something goes missing or gets lost.

All of the above might seem like too much, like hard work, but actually most of it needs doing at some point. It is only a little extra work but the effort is far outweighed by the loss if you do not take responsibility and it goes wrong.

Coaching

In Chapter 2, the point was made about understanding the limitations of your structure. This also goes for understanding the limitations of your coach and you need to take at least some of the responsibility for your development. Often coaches have more than one athlete to worry about; some have whole teams. Focusing on many people at once is difficult and generally, coaches manage the exceptions. The people at the top of the scale and at the bottom get the most attention and the people in the middle fall in the middle. It is a well-known rule called the Pareto Principle, or the 80/20 rule, (covered in more detail later). Roughly speaking, 80% of the attention will go to 20% of the people. The coach has to apply their focus somewhere and they will focus it where the greatest gains are (or biggest problems). Nevertheless, this is not a hard and fast rule that cannot be broken. It is just a natural way of things. However, by understanding this and taking responsibility yourself, you can break it. You do not have to be one of the problems or even the stars. You just need to take an interest in your development. I have not met a single coach who would not or has not welcomed this from the people they coach. Most will respond to an athlete's needs. If you take an interest in your development and are having an input, your coach will respond to that and work with you, spend a little more time. There is no one who puts you first more than you do.

"The most important job you have (as a coach) is growing your people, giving them a chance to reach their dreams." - Jack Welch, former CEO of General Electric (1935 - present)

The important thing is to talk to your coach. Do not assume anything. Do not assume that they know exactly what you want, what your aims and targets are. Do not even assume that they will tell you if they are not happy with something. Sometimes individuals have to make sacrifices for the team. You might be making a sacrifice for the team, but not even know it. Alternatively your coach might think that you have fantastic potential but that you do not want it badly enough. How does he/she know you want it? Coaches have to be careful not to push you harder than you can be pushed. If you do not show them what you want, they cannot help you get there.

Here is one final, and possibly controversial, word on coaches. Reading this, you are likely to be good at your sport and you are aiming high. You need to consider if you are in the right place to achieve that. In Chapter 15 I will explain about setting yourself up to fail for improvement, but, more generally, you need to objectively consider if your coach is pushing you forward or holding you back, intentionally or unintentionally. If you are the star player for your team, is your coach happy to push you on to another club that will make you better? Or, if your coach believes that they are the best person to bring you on, is that hubris? There is a certain amount of pride in bringing along an athlete to the highest level, but will that cloud the judgement of the coach? It is a special coach that will put in years of hard work with an athlete and then hand them over to someone else to refine and take the "glory" of finishing the job and getting the accolades. How many Olympians thank their old coach for what they have achieved rather than their current one? Generally, a coach will want the best for their athletes or team, but that will be from their own perspective. You need to take that decision for them. Do not be fickle, but, on the other hand, do not be afraid to make the leap either.

Taking a decision like that can be hard, but it is necessary and usually will have to be done at some point. Very few coach/athlete relationships last as long as former World Record holder and Olympic Gold medal-winning Sebastian Coe KBE and his father Peter or 2012 Olympic Gold medal winning heptathlete Jessica Ennis CBE and her coach Toni Minichello. Most athletes will have to move on to tougher or more competitive places. Maybe it is just that you have learned and developed as much as you can and it is now time to move on to a new challenge. It might even be that the training group you are with is no longer working for you. It might even be that you need nothing more than a fresh start, a new perspective.

"Things do not happen. Things are made to happen." - John F Kennedy (1917-1963) US President

When the time comes, you need to handle it properly. You should understand that, no matter what the circumstances that have led to the change, a coach has invested time and effort into your development. Be up front and honest with them. Be gracious and courteous, no matter how they react, thank them for their time and effort. Do not burn any bridges. You never know, you might be making a mistake. Do not lie to them to make it “easier”. It might seem easier to tell them that you want to try something new and are planning to come back, but it is always better to be completely honest. Explain your reasons, say your thanks, shake hands and move on.

Although that might seem a great deal of information about coaches, they are an important part of your development and as such they need special mention.

"Whether I fail or succeed shall be no man's doing but my own. I am the force. I can clear any obstacle before me or I can be lost in the maze. My choice; my responsibility; win or lose, only I hold the keys to my destiny." -Elaine Maxwell (Present) US Author

Practice

"My hunger is not for success, it is for excellence. Because when you attain excellence, success just naturally follows." - Mike Krzyzewski, Coach of US National Basketball Team (1947-present)

If you are to be successful in your chosen sport, practice is everything. But not just any practice. Firstly, the old axiom "Practice makes perfect" is wrong. "Practice makes permanent" is more accurate and therefore "Perfect practice makes perfect permanent" is more relevant. If your practice is sloppy, then you are wasting time and from a pure technical view, you are actually creating new and incorrect neural pathways for your body to follow. If you are supposed to be executing a practice at a particular level of effort, only you know for sure whether you are doing that. You are responsible for the execution, no one else.

"If your ship doesn't come in, swim out to it." - Jonathan Winters (1925-2013) US Comedian, Author, Actor and Artist.

Secondly, there is the principle of purposeful practice, described by Malcolm Gladwell in the first few chapters of Outliers based on K Anders Ericsson's research. This means that perfecting something is not enough. You have to continually push your practice so that it is challenging all the time. Not only do you have to learn the skills, you have to keep pushing the boundaries of them so that you are **always** struggling. You are forcing your body to adapt. Only you know where your effort level is and how far you can push, whether you are pushing your boundaries. Here is an extract from 'A Better Way to Train' by US Cycling Coach, Carl Cantrell

I had a woman racer who made all of my weekly lectures, rode the races, believed she was doing everything like I was telling her, and still couldn't improve on climbing.

I told her to go as hard as she could for short distances on the climbs to improve her climbing speed. She insisted that that was exactly what she was doing. Then, one day, I rode with her. Her perception of going as hard as she could was very different from what her body could actually do. She thought she was going as hard as she could and refused to believe otherwise. She could not grasp what sprinting really is.

Summary

Taking responsibility covers everything from being organised to your effort level in training. It's all about YOU. You are the one that needs to take responsibility for what happens to you and the sooner you start to, the sooner you will find that fewer things happen that take you by surprise.

1. Take responsibility both for the things you do and for the things that 'happen to you'.

2. See rule 1.

CHAPTER 9

THE 10,000 HOUR 'RULE'

"Talent is cheaper than table salt. What separates the talented individual from the successful is a lot of hard work" – Stephen King (1947-) Author

What is the 10,000 hour rule and why is it important? Unlike the other chapters in this book, this chapter is almost entirely about someone else's work. I will summarise the work of four other books, but it is worth getting all four books and reading them for yourself if you want to understand the 10,000 hour rule in more detail. The four books are Outliers by Malcolm Gladwell, The

Talent Code by Daniel Coyle, Bounce by Matthew Syed (all of which support the 10,000 hour rule) and The Sports Gene by David Epstein (which doesn't).

Talent is earned

The three books that support the 10,000 hour rule seek to debunk the theory that there is such a thing as natural talent. They claim that there is no God-given ability to perform in particular sports and that no-one is born with ability, despite what the newspapers may tell us. The only things that are genetic are the physical shape and size you have. Talent is hard-earned through practice, and to become world class takes roughly 10,000 hours. But not only does not everyone agree, there are very compelling reasons why this isn't the case.

Firstly, you need to understand that there are some definitions in the scientific community which might not be applied by writers and this can be confusing.

1. A hypothesis is an 'idea' that is used to explain observations; it must be testable and it must be able to make predictions about what would happen in similar situations so that it can be either verified or refuted.

2. A theory in science is a hypothesis that has withstood all attempts to falsify it. A 'theory' must have never been shown to be false despite thousands of attempts to break it. Although this might sound odd and slightly negative to a non-scientist, a scientist will welcome attempts to break their hypothesis and will attempt to do so themselves. Scientific papers are

published to allow others to test the hypothesis. This is because science is about discovery.

3. A rule (or law) is a theory that is well understood and extremely unlikely to ever be contradicted by additional data.

The above descriptions are important because authors and sometimes even Sports Scientists can mix scientific definitions with 'everyday' definitions and these mean you can come to believe things that are incorrect. It is because of this that I have put the term 'rule' into inverted commas in the title of this chapter. Although I will continue to refer to it this way as that is how it is commonly known, it is at best a hypothesis. David Epstein shows plenty of exceptions to the 'rule' which straight away cause it to fall foul of both the definition above of a hypothesis, never mind the definition of a theory, and certainly should prevent it from being called a rule. In fact, the original study that led Gladwell to the 10,000 hours rule by K Anders Ericsson showed that, while the best violinists (the original subjects of Ericsson's study) spent a remarkably large number of hours in solo practice, 10,000 hours was the *average.* Again, if you are dealing with averages, then there could be (and were) very high variations from the lowest to the highest, meaning that the hypothesis does not stand up to scientific scrutiny. It is worth noting, though, that Ericsson never proposed that '10,000 hours' was a rule or a theory.

So Gladwell and the books that followed from Coyle and Syed were founded on an error in interpretation. Further, Epstein's book shows that, in many cases, genetics mean that there are significant barriers to some people for sports. If you are not genetically predisposed to those sports, then you will never be elite no matter how much you practice. So, if the 10,000 hour rule is based on an error that even the lead researcher on the original study, K. Anders Ericsson discounts, then why is it important to you? If you have to be genetically wired to be elite in a particular sport, there is no point starting is there? This is where the definitions above are still important. Just as the 10,000 hour rule isn't a rule, we have enough exceptions to call foul on any theory at the moment that tells you that you cannot achieve what you set out to achieve including the genetic rules that Epstein covers in his book.

In his cycling manual, 'A Better Way to Train', Carl Cantrell gives the reader this exercise.

I am going to give you a homework assignment. I want you to write a five- page essay providing the scientific evidence that proves beyond any doubt that YOU cannot win the World Championships, Tour de France, or any other event that you would like to win. I want you to research what it would take to scientifically prove beyond any doubt that YOU cannot achieve your desired goals, no matter how big or how small they are.

What you will find is that we don't even know enough about the function of the human body and mind as an athlete to be able to prove that any individual person cannot achieve their desired goals.

In spite of this, there are many Exercise Physiologists who THINK they can determine which

athletes can and cannot win. They have their little rules, which they believe can prove who can and cannot be a champion in any sport. But, what they often fail to realize is that, for every one of their rules, we can show them exceptions to that rule.

There are sufficient studies in the three books mentioned above that identify that the primary natural talent is a deep love of the sport (or any other discipline) that leads to long and regular practice. Many studies have found that not only is hard and continuous practice required to achieve world class status, but that there were no world class performers who had not put in the work, no “naturals” who had a “shoo-in”. So far I haven’t seen evidence of any sedentary people suddenly being top class athletes although Epstein’s book comes close.

However, do you want to risk it? To do nothing and hope for the best? I thought not. Also, there is no-one who puts in the right quality and type of practice who does not achieve the highest level, although there is a great deal of debate about this also. I have found the same thing in all the biographies of successful people I have read. In the example of a study on the Berlin Academy of music by psychologist K. Anders Eriksson, described in Outliers, Eriksson could find no ‘naturals’ who were at the top of their class with less practice than others, no ‘grinds’ who worked as hard as the others in the elite but did not have what it takes. This can be countered by the argument that sport, unlike music, relies on genetic physical differences. It is my belief though that this may make the difference between being an Olympian and winning a gold medal, but that is all. It is only work that will put you in that contention and today's glass ceiling may not be there tomorrow when it comes to the physical limitations. Reading Epstein's book may tell us that there are particular genetic markers that suggest certain aptitudes, but so far so little is known about genetics, that they really don't tell you much at all.

There is one very important characteristic that is relevant for you and ties all the theories together. That is that in Ericsson's study, the people were already violinists, so he was comparing one violinist to another. This means they had already been pre-selected, non-violinists had been filtered out. That is why I am using the 10,000 hour rule here. You are already pre-selected because you have bought this book to improve in your sport. So you are already a sportsman/woman. You are not some sedentary couch potato, otherwise your chances are a little more distant. The other thing is, 10,000 hours just means 'a long time' or 'a huge amount of practice'. It is a notional number. In Gladwell's book it is equivalent of 10 years. So at this point, whether you achieve an elite level in 10 years or 7 or 13, does it make a difference now? I don't think so. 10,000 hours is 'good enough' for our purposes.

"The fight is won or lost far away from witnesses - behind the lines, in the gym and out there on the road, long before I dance under those lights." – Mohammed Ali (1942-) Former professional boxer and considered by many as the greatest heavyweight of all time.

The Only Place that Success comes before Work is in a Dictionary

"Work ethic must exceed the expectation level." - Tom Coughlin, Head Coach New York Giants US Football. ((1946 - present)

What this means is that to get to the top you have no choice but to put in the work, without exception. However, does that mean that if you put in the work, you will therefore get to the top? Actually no, there are two more factors that lead to becoming world class, the first being a deep love of the sport that generates the level of practice that means practicing or playing every waking moment. Think of the numbers. If you practice 2 hours every single day of the week and 4 hours on Saturday and Sunday, every single week of the year except for the two weeks that you are on holiday, you will have practiced 18 hours a week or 900 hours a year. To get to 10,000 hours you will have to maintain that for a further **11 years**. The 10,000 hour practise time has been found to work, on average and in general terms, for any major game, sport or other discipline (such as piano, guitar, chess). That first factor, the deep love of the sport that leads to the level of practice, is very significant, as few will have the love and the discipline to keep that up for that length of time. There are only a few percent of people in the world who have that desire, so straight away the quantity of people who will be in contention is automatically reduced. Here is a quote from Andre Agassi, winner of 60 Grand Prix Tennis titles including 8 Grand Slams and 1 Olympic gold, in his autobiography, Open.

"My father says that if I hit 2500 balls each day, I'll hit 17,500 balls each week and at the end of one year I'll have hit nearly one million balls. He believes in math. Numbers, he says, do not lie. A child who hits one million balls each year will be unbeatable."

"Natural talent only determines the limits of our athletic potential. It is dedication and discipline in your life that makes you great" – Billie Jean King (1942-) Former World Number 1 Tennis Player

Limitations and Obstacles

The second factor is that there tends to be a set of circumstances that are required to maintain, support and enable the progression from practice to world class. These sets of circumstances can initially seem quite random.

When you are born is a very significant factor. There are numerous studies in the books described regarding birth date, but to summarise, there is a distinct advantage to being born just after the cut off time than just before it for your given sport. Most sports in the UK follow school years and therefore the cut off date from one age to the next is 31 August. So if you are born on the 31 August you will be the youngest player in your age group.

Being born on 01 September means being the oldest in your age group. Think how significant that might be. If you are almost a year older than some of your contemporaries, in both physical and mental or emotional development then you are going to stand out. I was born at the end of August but it never once occurred to me that I might be at a disadvantage. I believed that in sport you either had talent or you didn't. I didn't. We had a footballer at our school who was very good, had trials at a number of clubs and went on to play in the English Premier League. He had natural talent. It was just a coincidence he was born in September, 11 months earlier than me, wasn't it?

The advantages to be gained in the early stages are huge because they are cumulative. The better you are, the more opportunity you get to play, the more chance you get to play for the district or play in the area championships, the national championships. Not only do you get more opportunity, but you are up against better competition. You get the impetus to do better, you get a taste for each higher level and that spurs you on. This means that the older kids get picked out early and get nurtured more. This phenomenon is well known and is referred to in psychology as 'cumulative advantage'.

If you are not sure this is true take this example from my own current discipline, track and field athletics. I will pick the first one because it's what my own son races, but you can do a similar study yourself. In the UK Under 17 men's 400m for 2012, for men born between 01 September 1995 and 31 August 1996, the age distribution in the top 100 performers (of the ones whose date of birth was visible) on the McCain Power of 10 database is as follows: athletes born in the first quarter (September, October, November) is 32; second quarter (December, January, February) is 19; third quarter (march, April, May) is 13; Last quarter (June, July, August) is 8. The distribution is highly skewed to the athletes born closest to the cut off date of August 31.

You will find a similar distribution in all sports, at all ages. If you are still not convinced then here, from the same database, is the under 15 women's shotput, 01 September 1997 to 31 August 1998 birth years, different sex, different type of event and different age group. Quarter 1 is 32; quarter 2 is 12, quarter 3 is 11; quarter 4 is 4. Read the books, do the research yourself. The date you were born has a huge impact on your comparison to your peers. The development advantage due to age levels out after puberty if all other factors are equal, but by this time the cumulative advantage gained by the older age group will have had an effect.

Another circumstance is location. It might be that you just happen to be close to where one of the high performance centres for a particular sport is. This generates interest in its own right as people in the area are achieving, which attracts others to participate. It also attracts coaches, facilities, sponsorship and support. This means you will be attracted to the sport and will then have the opportunity to perform at the highest level because the structure is there to support you. There are also other circumstances such as the natural environment. In a most extreme example, being born in either the area of Bekoji in Ethiopia or Iten in the Rift Valley in Kenya results in a set of conditions of diet, altitude and circumstances that will enable anyone with a middle or long distance running persuasion to develop particularly well. Additionally, as there are many champion athletes from these villages, everyone wants to be a runner. This increases the selection capability tremendously.

Additionally, you need the support. Whether from parents or someone close, there is always someone who has to provide the support, whether financial or otherwise to make sure you get the opportunities that you need; transporting you, paying for your coaching etc. Christian Malcolm, the four-time Olympian at 200m said his mum used to walk with him to and from the track, an hour each way, when he was too young to go on his own. That's the kind of support I'm talking about.

Lastly, you will need what is commonly termed as luck (In Chapter 20 I will cover luck further). In some cases this is a set of circumstances that come together to enable you to become world class. In a non-sporting sense, in Outliers, Gladwell describes the circumstances that gave Steve Jobs the opportunity to create Apple: living in Silicon Valley, at exactly the right time and with exactly the right set of opportunities. Or Bill Gates, being born near a school that could afford to be at the forefront of computer technology and having access to the computers and other programmers, again at exactly the right time, to enable the knowledge development that eventually led to Microsoft.

Sport is also subject to the same set of unique circumstances that come together to enable an athlete to combine the love of a sport, with the opportunities to progress that create a world class performer. So, if you are not born at exactly the right time, with a love of your particular sport, with the unique set of circumstances that allow you to develop, with a supportive family then you might as well give up now, right? This book would be less than satisfactory if it all ended there. If you are a competitor, then you are not going to let a few obstacles hold you back. Knowledge is power. Rather than accepting that there is nothing that can be done, knowing that there is no such thing as natural talent and that all talent is earned is empowering. If everything else is equal, you now know you can work your way to the top in 10,000 hours. Now you just need to level the playing field.

"What you don't know is how hard it is to make it look so easy." - Rascal Flatts, Rock Group

First, the practice and commitment has already been covered but it bears repeating that the practice must be always striving to improve, throughout the 10,000 hours. Quantity is not sufficient, quality is critical. I have driven for around 10,000 hours in the last 5 years alone (I have been driving around this level for around 20 years). Am I world class? Not even close. This is because my level of practice stabilised after the first year or so and then from that point on I have hardly improved; some would say I have got worse. This is because there has been no change in difficulty, no progress. I am not pushing myself to get better or testing myself. In a nutshell I am not striving for improvement so I am not improving.

"Successful people are not gifted; they just work hard, then succeed on purpose." - *G.K. Nielson*

But what about the things that you cannot control? You cannot control when and where you were born, where you live in your early years and whether your parents have enough money to support you.

"Impossible is just an opinion" – Deepak Chopra (1947-) US Physician and Alternative Medicine Practitioner

Location

Use what you have to your advantage. It might be that you do not have the perfect conditions, but you can adapt your surroundings to suit you. That is not to say that you can suddenly create a black run ski slope in your back yard. It is unlikely however, that if you live in central Birmingham you have decided to be an Olympic skier. You are already good at something and you want to get to the top, so whatever sport you are practising, you already have some level of skill and now you need to take it to the next level. Make your location work for you, get back to first principles; what is it that makes other people's location an advantage over yours, what are they getting out of it? It is not always what you think. Some of the best talent hotbeds spring up in the lowliest of places without the facilities that you would expect. Do not be distracted by shiny baubles, such as fancy gyms and spanking new equipment.

Find the coach who is getting results or who is prepared to work with you to get what you want. They are out there. Find somewhere that will replicate what you need; there is usually a way if you are creative enough.

Support

If you have not got the support, create it. If for whatever reason your parents cannot or will not support you, then find it elsewhere. If you are committed and disciplined (and appreciative) then there will be people who will support you if you look hard enough. I have known coaches go to extraordinary lengths to support kids who needed it when their parents could not or would not.

Creating Luck

As for luck, you make your own. You need to create the opportunities. It looks like Steve Jobs had extraordinary luck. But looking deeper, he put himself in the positions to become 'lucky'. It might be the case that he was born in Silicon Valley, but that, in my opinion, only led to what he was successful at, not whether he was successful. He got himself to talks outside of school; he followed up those talks by talking to the speakers afterwards to gain even more knowledge. In Outliers, Gladwell quotes this extract from one of the biographies on Jobs:

"(He) attended talks by Hewlett Packard scientists. The talks were about the latest advances in electronics and Jobs, exercising a style that was a trademark of his personality, collared the Hewlett Packard engineers and drew additional information from them. Once he even called Bill Hewlett, one of the company's founders, to request parts. Jobs not only received the parts he'd asked for but also managed to wrangle a summer job."

He pushed himself forward, eventually speaking to Bill Hewlett, which gave him an incredible opportunity to develop. That is not luck. You need to follow the same principle. We do not know how many people Jobs spoke to over the course of those talks or how long he spent learning, but it is likely that it was a lot more than is reported and that those people talked to each other. By the time Jobs talked to him, Hewlett probably already knew of Jobs, which made him more open to give him the opportunity. You may have to plant a lot of acorns for a long time before an oak tree starts to grow. You cannot afford to be shy and you cannot afford to waste an opportunity.

"Luck is what happens at the intersection of preparation and opportunity." - Jeff Fisher, US Football Coach, St Louis Rams (1958 - present)

From my own experience, when I attend sports events I do not spend time with my athletes (I specifically force them to be independent at meets as I cannot always be there and they need to learn how to look after themselves). Because of this it is not obvious to anyone who I am or who my athletes are and this means I get to overhear what people say about them and how much people discuss other people. Not just athletes talking, but coaches and parents. It is fascinating to listen to how other people talk about people you know. The first thing to understand is that people talk about other people. People they've seen, people they've met. News travels fast, far and wide; build on it. You have to push yourself forward. It is easier not to engage someone than it is to say no to them. If you ask for something and the person you are asking says no, then you are in no worse position than if you hadn't asked in the first place.

Happy Birthday

The one thing you cannot control is the date of your birth and if you're born at the wrong time; there can be a significant impact of your competitors being almost 12 months older than you. But knowing that they have that advantage and knowing that it is only a freak of birth that gives it to them, enables you to work around it. Knowing this may mean it takes you longer to hit the top echelon of your sport and that you have to work harder and push yourself forward into opportunities, but long term, it can be an advantage.

"The tougher my opponents, the more they present me with an opportunity to live up to my full potential and play my best." - Pete Carroll, Head Coach Seattle Seahawks US Football (1951 - present)

When you get to 15 or 16, it all starts to settle down and if you are still there and fighting your corner at that point, then you have a great chance, no matter what has happened in your earlier development. This is because the kids with the age (and development) advantage often become complacent and are unable to respond later to the kids that have had to work extremely hard to be on level terms. Suddenly, when developmentally everyone is in the same place and the age advantage is taken away, the hard workers continue to fly on. Also, the older kids are just not mentally prepared for not being the best anymore and get fed up and quit.

However, if you are one of the "morning stars", the kids that have the age advantage and are better than your peers at an early age, then the maxim "if you want to be number one, you have to train like you're number two" rings true. Use your early performances to your advantage but know that developmentally you will get caught up if you do not train as hard as the people chasing you. If you are a later developer, do not get disillusioned. You are just on a longer program, but the target for almost all sports is to become elite when you are an adult. What happens before that is just the journey, and this is covered in detail in Chapter 16. As I said earlier in the chapter, my son runs 400m. He is born in June, which puts him firmly at a disadvantage in the last quarter of the qualification year. However, I had done my research and drummed into him that if he kept going, then once everything settles down at the end of the under 17 age group, if he was still in there fighting, then he would have a great chance. With all credit to him, that is exactly what he did and coming out of the last Under 17 season (at the time of writing) he is 2nd in the UK after working slowly up the rankings over the last few years. It is possible, it just takes longer if you start at a disadvantage.

"Just keep going. Everybody gets better if they keep at it." -Ted Williams (1918-2002) US Baseball player

Summary

The 10,000 hours of purposeful practice is important, as are all the opportunities and circumstances required to get to the top, but now you know what the 'rules' are, you can work with them to get there. It doesn't matter where you are starting from, there will be a point for everyone when progress is slow and difficult, it just happens at different times. For some it will be at the beginning, for some it will be later on, but everyone will experience a stage where they have to grind through; no-one escapes unscathed. As for the genetic differences? Sure, there are people who have an advantage, but it is just another obstacle. There are exceptions, there are always exceptions. If you want it badly enough, don't let anyone tell you that you cannot be an exception like the exceptions that have gone before you. Lastly, what is an obstacle today may not be an obstacle tomorrow. There are always new ways of training, of executing a move, or of being good at a sport. Today's obstacles are only relevant in short-focus. Maybe you'll be the next Dick Fosbury (the high-jumper who transformed the sport with the 'Fosbury Flop') who changes how everyone approaches a particular sport. Never let anyone tell you that you cannot.

1. Read at least one of the recommended books so you understand the importance of proper, purposeful practice.

2. Overcome your circumstances.

3. Use what you do have to your advantage.

4. Play the long game. Do not sweat being a mid-table competitor at a young age. It is the end result that matters.

CHAPTER 10

TRAIN LIKE A CHAMPION

To be an elite athlete, in any sport, you need to have particular character traits. I have already covered the burning desire to be the best you can be, but there is also self-motivation, self-discipline, a slight obsessive-compulsive character concerning aspects of training, a high tolerance for pain and sacrifice and so on. A business coach once told me that it does not matter where an orange is, when you peel it, it is still an orange inside. The point they were making is that you cannot successfully maintain a different professional persona from your regular character. You are you, no matter where you are and what you are doing.

How do they do that?

What this means for you is that if you need to be all these things to become an elite athlete, then that is what you have to be. You cannot ‘act’ the part; you have to be that way. If you are sloppy and disorganised in your schoolwork then you cannot be acting the way you need to as an athlete.

“You have to put in many, many, many tiny efforts that nobody sees or appreciates before you achieve anything worthwhile.” - Brain Tracy, Canadian Public Speaker and Author (present)

You cannot afford to be anything other than focused and self disciplined or allow any seepage from a less committed version of you into your sporting life. If you do, you will find that you are ill-prepared, get injured, are late to training, miss games and so on. The better your coach and your training group, the less likely that this will be tolerated and you will find suddenly, you are no longer part of that training group any more. Greg Rutherford MBE, the Olympic Gold Medal winner in the Long Jump in 2012 was almost ejected from his group in his early years by his coach Tom McNab for his “reliability and punctuality”. If he had been, it is entirely possible that his journey would not have led to the Olympics. He is completely different now and trains very hard.

You have to have the same level of focus and discipline in everything you do. You have to be committed. That is not to say that you have to put the same time into everything, otherwise you will never hit your 10,000 hours in your sport. But if you are at school, then approach your school work the same way you approach your training. When you are doing it, give it everything you have, be 100% focused. Commit to it for the time you are doing it and then move on. Time is not refundable. You spend time. You may spend it wisely, or you may waste it, but it will keep passing whether you like it or not, all 86,400 seconds in the day.

Poor attention in other aspects of your life will affect your sport. If you do not put the effort in with your schoolwork then you might have to redo it, which is using up additional time you have not got to waste. You might get detention. You might even have to miss training to catch up. All because you were unable to put the effort and focus in when you should have done.

"We first make our habits, then our habits make us." - John Dryden, poet and playwright (1631 - 1700)

As for lateness and disorganisation in training, as a coach I hate it. Late comers are disruptive. If I'm 10 minutes into a warm up and I'm being asked by the late comers, “what are we doing, what’s next, what have I missed”, it means that one person is getting an unreasonable quantity of attention compared to the rest of the group for all the wrong reasons. “I’ve forgotten my spikes/boots/trainers, can I do something else”. What this says to me is that the athlete is not that interested. I cannot be more committed than the athlete themselves. I cannot do the reps and I will not be the one on the podium. If they are not committed in my mind, then my attention will go to athletes that are, regardless of ability. It might be that you are losing out just because of your disorganisation rather than a lack of interest, but take responsibility for your actions and the consequences.

Progression

To start to train like a champion you must be ready to start making some changes to how you train and practice, and to do this you should understand what a standard progression looks like for a normal athlete who plays sport. Initially, in your very early years, you play games at school, with your parents and with the kids of your parents’ friends. In your early years you will play one sport the most and that is dictated by one of three things:

- The sport that one of your parents did or is passionate about.
- The sport that is prevalent in the local area where you live.
- The sport that has the conditions to play where you grow up.

In other words, your parents may have been good at a particular sport and they push you in that direction either because they can support you or because they are living their dream through their child. This is not necessarily a negative thing, as they will be giving you a great start in a sport and you are doing purposeful practice from a young age. Many (but not all) sports stars start young, such as golfer Tiger Woods who started 'playing' golf at the age of two.

If you live in an area that lives and breathes football, such as Liverpool or Glasgow, then you are likely to play football from an early age. Alternatively, if you live on the coast in an area that has a very good junior section of a sailing club, you might end up getting into sailing early.

Formative Years

Getting into a sport at an early age can be an obvious advantage, however getting into any sport is also an advantage for almost any other sport. It is all preparation and it all counts and at a young age, most skills are transferable.

The next stage, during youth school years, is that through school Physical Education and after-school clubs and experimentation, you will try other sports. A vast majority of good sportsmen tend to be good at many sports. The basics of all physical sports are similar. They all involve a degree of the five components of athleticism defined by the IAAF (The International Association of Athletics Federations) – strength, speed, stamina, suppleness and skill. The difference tends to be mainly in technique (skill); the other components exist in different balances. Trying different sports is important because most sports, if only followed in their pure form, are very specialised. However, the top 5% of the players need more than just the skills and fitness levels their own sports give them. Kelvin Giles, of Movement Dynamics, created a system of "Physical Competence" and states that to be World Class at a sport requires the elimination of physical weaknesses. This is not just in the particular sport, but the removal of all physical weakness for all sports. Many professional sports recognise this. Teams do camps where they learn other sports to improve their play, football players learn martial arts, boxers learn ballet, pole-vaulters do gymnastics.

During these youth years, doing the extra work is important. So much so that British Athletics has introduced a program called Athletics 365, which is aimed at delivering the first four of the components of athleticism for any sport including all the different physical attributes that juniors should have; balance, coordination, agility, flexibility and the ability to run, jump and throw correctly.

Loren Seagrave, the creator of Speed Dynamics and Velocity Sports Performance, calls the ages between 7-12 the skill-hungry years, where kids are developing neural pathways very quickly and can learn new skills at an incredible rate. It is during this period that the biggest gains can be made. It is much better to learn as many skills as possible during these years than by trying a 2-week training camp in later life. Sophie Hitchon, the British Hammer Thrower and 2012 Olympic Finallist, was originally a ballerina which she says gave her great balance and posture.

"Success is nothing more than a few simple disciplines, practiced every day." - Jim Rohn (1930-2009) US entrepreneur, author and motivational speaker

For example, if you tried to picture the “perfect ” footballer, they may have the endurance and physique of a swimmer, the speed of a sprinter, the grace, balance and explosiveness of a gymnast as well as the technical skills of a footballer. Many advanced sports are recognising this and are targeting the overall athleticism that is required in the early years. You might be reading this at a later age, but it’s never too late to start. Look at the attributes you need to be the full package and find out which sports or disciplines do those best and go out and learn from them. If you are still young enough, diversify now. It will benefit you greatly in the long run.

Specialisation

Before I cover specialisation, let me say that I can’t stress enough that early specialisation can do more to damage your long term success than anything else. I’ve covered the benefits of achieving all round athleticism above and the avoidance of injury in the next chapter. Both of these are at risk when a child specialises in a sport at an early age at the exclusion of everything else. My advice is that a child should no specialise in a particular sport until at least 15 and in an event or position until at least 17. That might sound high risk, but think about team sports, where kids are stuck in goal at football or hockey and never get chance to play on the pitch. How many are still playing into adult ages? Often, great goalkeepers can play on the field as well as in goal. There's a reason that's the case.

However, after the youth phase, you will probably have locked in on a sport. You will have tried quite a few, probably found you were good at most but decided you liked one best. It is not necessarily the one you started out in, but that does not matter. This specialisation doesn't necessarily have to happen now and in some cases it doesn't matter until later, but you will specialise at some point. Now that you have chosen your sport, you need to get good at it. Not the 'good' that is compared to your peers. You need to get really good compared to the people that you want to compete with. You need to start moving towards your dream. At whatever level you are at, you need to find out what it takes to get to the next level.

There are some people who believe that trying to follow the training program of someone who is elite, when you are not elite, is folly and that it will not work for you. These people will say that the person you are imitating did not train like that when they were at your level, and therefore neither should you. There is an element of truth in this, but only insofar as you need to understand your training and development capacity. In many cases, the athletes who you are aspiring to emulate have learned from trial and error or have stepped up their training as they move through the tiers of performance. As you move up the ladder, the competition gets harder and you have to prepare more, work harder, and take care of the smaller things. The margins of success and failure are smaller so the gains are smaller.

"If you only ever give 90% in training then you will only ever give 90% when it matters." -Michael Owen (1979-) Former England Football Player

Think about this for a moment. At some point in the future, you will step up your level of training and all the things that go with it when you need to maintain the new performance level. Revisit the chapter on responsibility. Who are you waiting to tell you that you need to do more? If you have read about or researched one of the stars, and they are doing a certain level of training, then what is stopping you from doing the same? That is not to say that you need to do the same level of intensity as the elite performers and your coach (and possibly a doctor) will need to advise you on this, but it is the level of commitment that they have that can be imitated. If you run track and you follow the running program provided by your coach then you will be fine. But if you read that Mo Farah not only trains track, but runs on the road, does lots of conditioning work, weights and flexibility then ask yourself why you aren't doing that. You may not be able to run the miles or the speeds or even lift the same weights, but as a general program, you *can* cover the areas that he covers.

"I've met only a couple of people that I feel were more physically talented or naturally gifted than I am. I've only met a couple of people who I feel probably worked harder than me. But I've never met anyone that I felt has both of those." - Daley Thomson (1958-) Former Olympic Decathlete and World Record Holder

It might even be that, as far as you know, you are doing what everyone in your sport does, elite performers included, but that in other sports with similar requirements, they do something different. Why is that? Before British Cycling changed the rules, cyclists never used to cool down. Only when the team recruited a sport scientist from British Swimming did they start and everyone else followed suit quickly.

In his book The Sport Gene, David Epstein shows that different people respond to training in different ways because they are genetically programmed to do so. If everyone in your training group is doing the same things, then some will respond better than others and improve more. This doesn't mean that some people are just working harder than others, it is that they are just programmed to respond differently. You need to find what works for you. Not about what feels comfortable, but what actually generates improvement in a measurable way.

One thing to understand is that certain training intensity levels, and volumes are not possible without other supporting disciplines such as nutrition, hydration and recovery. The full detail of this is beyond the scope of this book, but as you move up the ladder, the "whole package" is a lot bigger than it first appears and I have included a basic guide in Appendix 1.

"I've got a theory that if you give 100% all of the time, somehow things will work out in the end." - Larry Bird (1956-) Former NBA Basketball player and coach.

A New Level

In your own sport, how good are the people you are emulating? Even though you know your sport fairly well, especially if you have done your research, you probably can't reconcile how much practice it takes to be good. In teenage years, most amateur football players in the UK will do 2-3 hours training per week and 1 game per week on average. How much progression do you think you can make in 2-3 hours per week? Most of the great players would practice skills over and over until they were perfect and permanent. Every free kick that David Beckham OBE takes will have been practiced from the same spot over and over again. It will be ingrained and repeatable. When you see Tiger Woods play a difficult shot in a championship, we marvel at how good he is. What you do not see is that he has probably played that very shot for more hours than a serious amateur golfer has played golf!

In his second autobiography “My Time”, Sir Bradley Wiggins, Tour de France and many time Olympic medallist, explained that “Even though I got close to the podium of the Tour (de France) in 2009, I’d say it was only in 2011 that I completely understood how much you need to work to get to the very top, what hard training is, and how much of a lifestyle change is involved. I simply didn’t train as much back then. I just never did the work. I’ve now realised what I am capable of and I’ve done something about it.”

“You can’t run in place or someone will pass you by. It does;t matter how many games you’ve won.” - Jim Valvano, US College Basketball coach and broadcaster (1946 - 1993)

Businessman and football coach Simon Clifford has recognised this with his Brazilian Soccer School where skills are practised repeatedly so that in a game they are so ingrained that they become natural. His system is the equivalent of martial arts where the movements are repeated faster and faster and more and more powerfully so that when executed in a bout, there is no thought or delay and the movement is accurate. Sprinters do running drills over and over again. Tennis players repeat the same shots, over and over.

Stages of Learning

To understand this better, it is worth understanding the stages involved in learning a new skill.

- Unconscious Incompetence – where you are unable to carry out a movement or skill and do not know how to.

- Conscious incompetence – where you can consider a skill, think about it, but are unable to execute it fully.

- Conscious competence – where you practice the move and can execute it with consideration and thought.

- Unconscious competence – where you execute a move without thought because you have practiced so much that it becomes 'natural'. This is where people will look at you and talk about your 'natural' ability. This is known as the 'Iceberg' effect. What people see is that you have a natural talent; they only see the tip of the iceberg. What they do not see is that you have practised and practised, over and over so that the movement or skill is ingrained in you and your body knows how to perform it.

Is gaining that skill as simple as practising it over and over again? Yes, and no. Yes, in that it is the key to achieving unconscious competence, but simply doing the same thing over and over again will not make you an expert. Remember practice only makes permanent.

Firstly, there are ways to practice that will achieve outstanding results. A coach is very useful because they have what is known as the 'coach's eye'. They have already done their practice and have a model in their head of what a move should look like and can compare what you do to that model. But you do not need a coach for everything. At some time in my coaching education, someone said to me that "there are no coaches in skate parks". Think about that for a moment. Go to a skate park. There are some incredible feats of very complex (and brave) skills. Where are the coaches that are getting the kids through this, helping them to learn? Why doesn't it take them long to learn?

You never stay the same. You either get better or you get worse." - Jon Gruden, former NFL Coach of the Oakland Raiders and Tampa Bay Buccaneers (1963-present)

The simple answer is that unconsciously they have latched onto an almost perfect method of learning skills. This method has been adopted by some sports and has led to the recognition that you should not over-coach. Verbal feedback from a coach is one of the least effective methods of learning, so it should always be part of some other method of feedback. A good coach will not tell you what you have done wrong and expect you to get it right next time. They will ask you questions, help you to discover the fault for yourself and then guide you to find the right way to correct it.

Secondly, the most important thing to note is that the skateboarders take ownership of their learning. They've decided to learn the skill so they will watch someone else perform the skill and study the movement closely. They will use their learned experience to start a process of breaking down the skill and comparing it to what they already know. If you take coaches out of the equation, the skills will be naturally progressive, the skills being learned becoming more difficult as each new one is mastered. Then the athlete, because that is what skateboarders are, will go through a series of methods to perfect the skill, not necessarily in the same order.

Methods of Learning

British Athletics uses the following terms to describe how skills are learned:

- "Whole – part – whole" – where the athlete attempts the movement, then picks a particular part, practises it until they can consciously execute it and then puts it back in to attempt the whole again.

- "Chaining" or "chunking" – involves breaking the movement down into smaller parts (a sequence) and practicing them in those parts, making sure each of the parts is locked in before trying to put the whole back together. As skateboarding has a very specific language that not everyone knows I will use a simpler example of a triple jump (or hop, step, jump) in track and field to explain this. In a triple jump, the athlete must run to a board at full speed, followed by a hop, then a step and then a jump into the pit. Chunking would involve practising each phase described independently. Practising and perfecting the run-up to get the correct speed into the board and to ensure the board is hit correctly and consistently. Then practising the hop, the step, the jump and the flight phases independently of each other so that each can be focused upon and perfected without the other phases being a distraction.

- Shaping – In shaping, the principle is to make the skill easier to practice and then make it progressively more difficult. In triple jump this might involve hop, step, jump from a standing start, then progressing to a 3 step run up, then a five step and so on. In football, it might be taking a free kick to a target and making the target progressively smaller or moving the target farther away.

Not every technique is appropriate or possible to use to learn every skill, but the skaters will naturally select the appropriate one at any given time or for a given skill. They will repeat and perfect, moving back and forward around the learning techniques until they have the skill embedded.

It is all practice and it is all necessary. If champions are training three times per day, six days per week, then why aren't you doing the same? Depending on where you are in your development, there might be good reason for not doing something, physically, medically or academically. Some things cannot be sacrificed. But if it is only about you and your Play Station or you and your Facebook account, then you might need to change your commitment level. If not you will need to change your expectation as I covered in detail in the chapter on Sacrifice.

"Time is non-refundable" Eric Thomas (Present) Renowned motivational speaker and author

Look at all the other aspects of elite training, the conditioning, nutrition, hydration, recovery. Everything that a champion or elite performer does is done for a reason. Nothing is left to chance. If you are not sure, then do more research.

"I've missed more than 9000 shots in my career. I've lost almost 300 games. 26 times, I've been trusted to take the game winning shot and missed. I've failed over and over and over again in my life. And that is why I succeed." Michael Jordan (1963-) NBA Basketball player and businessman, many believe to be the greatest player of all time

Summary

Never look at a champion and think that they are doing something that you can't. To get where they need to get to, they have practised and practised. They have made the same move many times in training. Natural talent is a myth. It actually belittles the amount of effort that an athlete has put in to get them to the top. Accept that hard work will bring reward and then use that to push yourself to work as hard as those champions have. Do not give up. Believe in yourself that you can do it and you will, it just may take longer than you thought, but at least it is possible. Look to the long haul. Which would you rather be, the best U13 football player in the league or an elite at 18?

1. Look at elite athletes in your sport and outside your sport and identify what they are doing differently to you and write them down.

2. Be objective in why you are not doing those things (remember that some things can not be sacrificed; e.g. education or health)

3. Introduce the appropriate parts from your list into your training – number of times per week, conditioning, nutrition, flexibility, recovery, and hydration. See appendix 1 for more details on the kinds of things covered here.

Chapter 11

Protection

When it comes to development and long term improvement, avoiding injury is one of the biggest performance enhancers there is. This might sounds strange, but avoidance of injury should take precedence over all other training and competition needs. This isn't an idle comment.

As a child grows and develops through normal puberty and general physical development, they will grow stronger and they will improve athletically. A boy of 15 will throw further than when he was 12, without any coaching intervention. There are many ways to get injured and it is sometimes unavoidable, especially in team sports. I will deal with how to manage injuries when they arise in a later chapter, but there are some injuries that are entirely avoidable and I will deal with these here.

Effect of an injury on development

I am fortunate to be part of the England Athletics National Coach Development Programme for Speed and during one of these sessions I spoke to Tony Hadley, the British Athletics Event Group Lead for Sprints. His view was that the one of the best ways to develop an elite athlete was to keep them injury-free for six macro-cycles (a macro-cycle is a large training period, in this instance a winter indoor season would be one, then a summer outdoor season would be a second and so on). This means three years free from injury.

The other thing the told me was that if an athlete has a significant injury, he believed it would take four macro-cycles (two years) from resuming training to return to their previous form. Obviously this isn't a hard and fast rule, but as a general principle, this informs the philosophy of elite coaches. The role of a coach (and parent or mentor) is not to drive the athlete to higher performances and push their development. That is the role of personal trainers and army drill instructors, who have no place in the development of a junior. A coach should ***enable*** you, the athlete to develop and they are the ones that must exercise patience, taking a long term view. They should look at the overall scheme, knowing that an extra repetition may not be worth the benefit.

Training Load

Something I have heard many times over my years as a coach (and something I now follow myself) is that a training programme should be the minimum load required to achieve the progression and no more. It is very difficult to develop a programme for a year's training and fit everything in. It is then harder still to the strip out the unnecessary workload on the athletes, because at first look, everything looks necessary.

"Simplify as much as possible. When you add, you must subtract." - Don Meyer, US College Basketball Coach (1944 - 2014)

A training programme needs to include all the elements of athletic development, the Five S - Speed, Strength, Suppleness, Stamina, Skill. With young athletes, trying to fit all these in is difficult. There is limited time available for training among the rest of your life. What the better-trained coaches do in this case is to identify where they can get multiple benefits from the same exercise. In my case for example (having learned from these better-trained coaches), my warm-up will have skill, strength and stamina elements. This means in one half hour slot, by controlling the intensity of the activities, the rest periods and the types of exercises done, I can achieve a huge amount of training, without overloading the athletes.

The reason training load is so important is that when athletes of any level and in any discipline become fatigued, they are at a higher risk of injury. Turning up for a training session in the evening after playing a rugby tournament at school all day, without telling your coach, creates a high risk of injury. When you are fatigued, your movement patterns change, but your body compensates. It starts to use other muscles. If those muscles aren't used to the movement or intensity, or aren't prepared correctly, injuries occur.

If you are playing in or training for multiple sports at a good competitive level, you need to discuss your training load with your coach. Make sure they are aware of what you are doing so they can make adaptions if necessary.

Warm Up

"The only secrets, if there are any, are good teaching of sound fundamentals." - Adolph Rupp 1901-1977, seen as one of the most successful coaches in American College Basketball

The warm up is a critical part of avoiding injuries but in many sports it is often neglected. Consider this; for a competition in warm conditions, my sprinters will warm up for an hour before competing. If it is colder, it will be longer. I have seen football teams at junior league level warm up by everyone crowding into the penalty box for a player to cross balls in for them to try to scramble, while they wait for the kick off. Is football different to sprinting in injury risk? Think of it this way. Football is a winter sport, so it's likely to be cold. Kick off comes around and the first thing a team will often do is punt the ball forward for one of the wings to chase. Suddenly, from a standing start on a cold day with no real preparation, the winger is into a flat-out sprint.

So what should a warm up look like? First it is important to understand the function of a warm up. It is to prepare the body for the event and intensity it is about to undertake. Prepare the body! Just getting warm isn't the sole function. It takes about 5 minutes from a standing start on a clement day to raise the body temperature sufficiently to start proper purposeful movement. Think about this for a moment. This would be the equivalent of four full laps of a football pitch **before** the functional warm up starts!

"Preparation can be defined in three words: Leave Nothing Undone." - George Allen, 1918-1990, US NFL Coach with the third best winning percentage in NFL history.

The next step would be to mobilise all the major joints. Most joints will be used in some way in most sports, whether as part of the activity or as part of the support and balance. Throwing a rugby ball might seem to be an arm movement, but every joint in the body will be involved in some form, so all of them have to be mobilised. A simple way to mobilise each joint is to rotate it to it's extremes in both directions (I use 10 rotations in each direction). I usually start from the bottom up - ankles, knees, hips, trunk, shoulders, elbows, wrists and then neck. Do not rotate the neck though. Head should go forward-back and side-side.

Now that the joints are mobile, dynamic stretching should then start. Never static stretch a cold muscle as again, this can cause injury. It is fine to do static stretching towards the end of a good warm-up, but never do this at the start. A dynamic stretch is an extended movement such as standing (or walking) and then extending up onto tiptoes and relaxing back down. Walking lunges, backward walking lunges, high-stepping and leg swings are all types of dynamic stretches. These should start at low intensity and build up in effort.

Once this is complete, we move onto more plyometric movements such as skipping. Then, the event or discipline movement patterns can start. These start at low intensity, usually 50% and will build up gradually to maximum intensity efforts. If you do a multi-movement sport such as tennis or hockey, then practise all the movement patterns at each intensity building up to full performance level.

Once you are warm, stay warm until it's time to compete. Stay well wrapped up and clothed until just before your event starts. Keep your tracksuit on, stay mobile and moving. If you warm up and then sit down for 15 minutes listening to a team talk, you will lose the benefit of the warm up. Stand up to listen and keep moving.

Energy systems and recovery

Training has different effects on different physical and neurological systems in the body and these have different recovery times. As I said earlier in the chapter, fatigue is often the enemy. But fatigue is not obvious if you don't know how your body responds to certain exercises.

For some exercise types (high intensity training such as maximum speed sprinting), your body needs to recover for 2 days before you should repeat the same type of exercise. For others, the fatigue effect doesn't even start for two days and then lasts for longer.

For example, very high intensity weight training (1-3 repetition loads) or maximum velocity sprinting does not particularly fatigue the muscular system and can be repeated a couple of hours later if necessary. However, the central nervous system (CNS) is fatigued and this has a physiological effect on the body and will take a minimum of 48 hours to recover from. That is correct, two days to recover from. However, this doesn't mean that you can't train, you just need to avoid CNS stress. Therefore on the next day, a lower intensity training session should be followed such as aerobic or distance training. It isn't just that you need to recover, but the next day's training cannot be effective. Studies have shown that when the CNS is fatigued, ground contact times are increased in sprinters, slower weight lifting speeds are achieved or with reduced weight capacity. If you are attempting a clean or a snatch with high weight when your CNS is fatigued, and this is performed slower than normal, you will be able to see how injury could easily occur.

Whether you wish to learn more about training theory and body system recovery or not, the rules are fairly simple. If you are fatigued, talk to your coach. There is (or should be) a specific purpose to every training session. If you are fatigued then you might have to modify what you do. Don't let your ego get in the way and try to tough it out if the session would be wasted. Remember the impact of an injury if you pick one up. Listen to your body. You can feel the difference in it. Does it feel like you can do what the training requires?

On the other hand, understand what fatigue is. It is a specific response to training. It is different from a lack of motivation, or being a bit tired. Don't use it as an excuse.

Technique

Mastering a technique is a vital part of avoiding injury. Too many people rush into movements or exercises without understanding the necessary technique required to perform the action correctly. Not only does this embed incorrect movement patterns (so-called muscle-memory) but it increases load on muscles that aren't supposed to be doing the movement.

"There is no point making a bad technique more efficient." - Lee Ness, Author and Coach

If you look at a seemingly "simple" technique such as a sit-up or a plank, incorrectly performing these exercises can create lower back problems. The very purpose of such an exercise - to improve core strength - becomes completely destroyed by an injury to the back.

Most so-called "overuse" injuries aren't overuse at all. They are simply a result of performing a movement incorrectly for long periods. Even running requires proper technique. Many running injuries and pains are caused by incorrect running mechanics. When repeated over many miles, these become chronic and then acute as the injury progresses. In some cases, the body becomes so adapted to the poor technique that the chronic condition becomes permanent, such as with over- or under-pronation. Early recognition and intervention at youth and junior level would prevent most long term injuries.

"The greatest mistake is to continue to practise a mistake." - Bobby Bowden, US College Football Coach, (1929 - present)

It is clear that technique is not only important for proper skill acquisition, but it is just as, if not more, important for injury prevention.

Flexibility

My last point on injury prevention is on flexibility, or suppleness in the Five S model. Many people incorrectly believe that big powerful muscles are bound to be inflexible. Not only is this not the case, but the opposite is true. In a study by the Clinical Journal in Sports Medicine it was found that increasing the range of motion in adults with tight hamstrings by performing hamstring stretches five days per week for six weeks, the thigh muscle strength increased.

Increasing flexibility, suppleness and range of motion is, like everything else, a focused skill. It will not be achieved by a few light stretches after a workout. Flexibility is a dedicated workout, with it's own objectives and measures. It has it's own specific techniques.

One important point, building on never stretching a cold muscle, is that a proper flexibility session is quite tiring if done correctly and creates fatigue. It shouldn't be done before a training session but can be done afterwards. If done as a stand-alone session, this should only follow a full warm up.

With flexibility stretching, I prefer to start at the core and work outwards. It is also useful to stretch opposing muscle groups in mini-sets, such as hamstrings, thigh, hamstrings, thigh, hamstrings, thigh before moving onto the next muscle pair.

Static stretching is the most common method of improving flexibility and if performed regularly will permanently improve range of motion. Static stretching involves gradually stretching the muscle to the point it tightens (not beyond) and then holding the stretch for 30 seconds. As the tight sensation subsides, you should push further into the stretch to maintain the tightness of the muscle. After relaxing the muscle this can be repeated a couple of times before moving onto the next muscle.

I find PNF stretching (Proprioceptive Neuromuscular Facilitation) is the most effective for maximum gains in flexibility. The initial stretch is similar to static stretch where you gradually move into the stretch until the focus muscle is tight. This is then held in this position for 10 seconds. At the end of the 10 seconds, you should push against the stretch at about 65% effort while in the same position (this requires a partner, an object or something like a towel) for a further 10 seconds. For example, if you are stretching your quadriceps by pulling your foot to your butt for 10 seconds, the second 10 seconds would be to hold this position, but try to straighten your leg against the resistance of you hand for the next 10). On relaxing, the stretch is then increased and the cycle repeated a further twice.

Summary

Proper training organisation at the long term level and proper warm ups before each activity is the best way to avoid avoidable injuries. Take responsibility for keeping your coach informed and listen to your body. Additionally, if your team doesn't do a proper warm-up, then create your own. Contact me if you like and I will send you one.

Competing season in, season out for years will benefit you far more than a single training session or event will. Understand the consequences of injury and take steps to avoid it.

Be aware of your training load and keep your coach informed of the other things you are doing.

Warm up correctly.

Avoid fatigue.

Learn the correct techniques for **every** movement.

Stretch.

CHAPTER 12

PHYSICAL PREPARATION

A competition is when all of your training and preparation come together to deliver a performance. There is no point in being the best in training if you cannot deliver when it matters. Just turning up on the day and hoping for the best is never going to cut it if you want to be an elite performer. If you do that, you are leaving too much to chance and you will see from Chapter 20 that luck is not something you should be prepared to rely on. The preparations for each sport will be different and there will also be significant differences between a team sport, where you compete every week, and an individual sport, where you might compete once every couple of months. The basics are similar though, and, certainly, mental preparation is crucial.

"The will to succeed is important, but what's more important is the will to prepare." -Bobby Knight (1940-) US Basketball Coach

The 5 P's

The first principle is to remove any stress from the day. Try to use the 5 P's: Prior Preparation Prevents Poor Performance. In Chapter 8 the emphasis was on taking responsibility for your own performances and the 5Ps are an extension of this. If you are well prepared, then on the day you are not worrying about things that you do not need to and this is going to help your performance. Have a routine because having a routine is relaxing in itself.

routine |roo͞ˈtēn|

noun

A sequence of actions regularly followed; a fixed program

Start by getting yourself organised early. If it is an event you have to enter, sort out a timeline that counts back from the event, such as:

• 6 weeks before – enter the event, make sure communication or entry is confirmed and that you have completed everything correctly.

• 2 weeks before – organise or confirm transport and accommodation. How are you getting there, how far in advance do you need to be there? Check train timetables and make sure there are no engineering works planned. If you have never been before, check the routes and how long everything takes.

• 1 week before – check event timings and any relevant rules. Timetables change close to events so check again. Are there specific rules you need to adhere to such as call-ups or signing in?

• 4 days before – make sure your kit is all laundered and ready. Not just your competition kit such as shoes or uniform, but your travelling kit, warm up kit, and any spares you need such as studs or spikes.

• 2 days before – Make sure you have everything you need in case you run out of something. This includes your food, cash, pins for race numbers etc. This gives you just enough time to get something if there is anything you have forgotten.

• 1 day before – pack all kit and double check everything. Lay it all out ready.
If you know you have everything covered, then you will

rest easy and have no reason to worry about anything unnecessarily. Like everything else, your routine should be practised and refined over time. Make a kit list so you can check everything off. Use a calendar as a reminder of when to do everything and tick it off when you do it. Even if you are competing every week, put together a weekly calendar and follow it. Remember, every game is important and being unprepared just because of carelessness may cost you a golden opportunity.

"One important key to success is self-confidence. An important key to self-confidence is preparation." - Arthur Ashe (1943-1993) World No. 1 Tennis Player from the US

Tapering

So, you have your admin sorted, you now need to make sure you are prepared physically. At this stage, as Latif Thomas, founder of Athletes Acceleration, Complete Track and Field and creator of Complete Speed Training, would say “The hay’s in the barn”. You have done everything you can; it’s now time to put it into effect. For athletes who are working towards a few big competitions in the year, rather than ones who compete every week, this will involve a ‘taper’. I will only cover the principles of tapering very briefly here, but I suggest further research if you do not know what it is and for you to talk to your coach about it if you have one. However, even athletes who are aware of tapering and whose coach plans in a taper can still have a tendency to screw it up because they don't understand it. I know of athletes who will override the taper their coach has planned by training without the coach's knowledge, mainly because they don't understand what a taper is.

Firstly, it is slightly counter-intuitive. To be fully prepared to be at your best you need to back off your training. For some this can start as long as 10 days out from a big competition. As an example and as a very rough rule of thumb (I use this as a guide but customise by athlete or competition) I do a rule of three. I treat the taper as three blocks of three days. My training programmes have patterns and routines so I will stick with the normal routine during the taper. I plan standard sessions as if there was no competition and then for the first three days I will reduce the volume by 25%. The second three days the volume will be reduced by 50%. The last three days will be almost nothing; practising routines, stretching, nothing exciting. Some people really struggle with a reduced training load. As mentioned earlier, they will do more or increase the intensity without the coach knowing.

The other problem with tapering is that sometimes you start to feel worse. Your training sessions become more of a struggle. Where previously you were hitting the numbers, you suddenly start to labour. At this point athletes start to panic and often they will jump off the taper and step up the training. But this struggle is a natural response. It is your body adapting. You might think that this cannot happen this quickly, but actually, your competition phase training is already high intensity and low volume before you hit your taper so your body is already adapting. So what is happening here?

If you take someone like a track athlete or swimmer who is training twice a day, six days a week through a long pre-season and into a peak competition phase, then for six months or more their body has been in a continuously fatigued state. They are recovering between sessions and coaches will balance which session follows what to spread the load across the body's energy and neural systems, but you are still training very regularly. Suddenly the training load starts to come off to where it is almost non-existent and your body makes the most of this by rebuilding everything. This is what the taper is for, but it takes a lot of energy for your body to do it, rebuilding cells at a molecular level. While this adaptation takes place, you may be slightly off compared to normal, but you need to let the process work.

If done right then you will come out of the taper without the fatigue, feeling fresh with every system rebuilt and fully operational. Clyde Hart, coach to four-time Olympic gold medallist and current 400m world record holder Michael Johnson, explained that when you are training you are putting money in the bank, you are building up your war chest ready for your competition. When you compete, you are taking money out. In a competition phase and especially a taper, you need to be very careful. Are you putting into the bank, or taking out?

Tried and Tested

You also need to make sure you look after yourself in the run up. Whether it is an important competition or just a weekly match, you need to make sure that whatever you do, you have done it before. Do not suddenly decide to try a new foreign food the night before a big game. Your eating and drinking routine should be tried and tested. It might be as simple as keeping away from new foods before you compete or it might be that you are an endurance athlete and you need to carbohydrate-load. This takes about a week and I will not cover it here, but it does not agree with everyone, so if you are going to do it, practice first! The morning of a competition needs to be the correct type of food, so does your feeding strategy through the competition if it goes on for long periods, but again, practice, practice, practice.

Staying hydrated during training should be second nature if you are a serious athlete as a 2.5% bodyweight loss of hydration can cause a 45% drop in performance. Hydration cannot be done in short order on the morning of a race though. Your body needs to build up and then maintain. Allow a week for full hydration. If you are on a taper, then be careful not to drop off your hydration too much. Some athletes will lose track of all sorts of things when their routine changes.

Get plenty of sleep in the run up to a big competition. Preparation might take a few days, it might be as high as ten, but getting plenty of sleep really allows the adaptation and full rebuilding to happen better. The more sleep and rest you get during a taper, the better. A lot of elite athletes in the taper period will try to sit rather than stand, or lie down, rather than sit. They do not even walk anywhere if they can help it. This is not laziness; it is allowing your body to work its magic preparing for the competition ahead.

Staying Healthy

Lastly, in terms of physical preparation, is staying free of illness. Eating healthily and topping up with a multi-vitamin will help, but it is worth taking extra steps if the competition is very important. There can be nothing worse than preparing for a year for a specific competition and then coming down with a cold. So how do you avoid a cold? As ever don't trust to luck because you can take a bit more control. Elite athletes in the run up to a world championship, Olympics or an event like the Tour de France will segregate themselves in camps with doctors on hand. Obviously it is unlikely that you will have that level of support, but the single highest cause of infections is from the hands. If you want to greatly reduce your chances of catching cold or another illness you need to keep on top of your hand hygiene. Allow yourself to become a little obsessive with it. Wash your hands regularly and thoroughly. Carry a bottle of hand sanitizer. Use it whenever you touch anything. Think of it this way, when most people sneeze, they do so into their hands. Anything they then touch can carry an infection. Door handles, banisters, you. You can then pick that up and if you do not clean it, the infection can find a nice new host in you. So keep your hands clean in the run up to competition.

Summary

Training for weeks, months or years for an event can be wasted if you are not physically prepared. Make sure you have all your preparation routines practised and in place so that you can arrive at any event healthy, ready and in peak condition.

1. Practise a pre-competition routine and stick to it (do not introduce anything new in a competition phase, such as new food).

2. If your competition schedule is irregular or intermittent (as opposed to playing matches every week) then understand how tapers work and practise them.

3. Practise your feeding routine and stick to it.

4. Hydrate properly for a week ahead of a big competition (or, preferably, take care of your hydration all the time!)

5. Get plenty of rest in the week before a competition, especially if you are prone to sleeplessness the night before.

6. Keep your hands clean!

CHAPTER 13

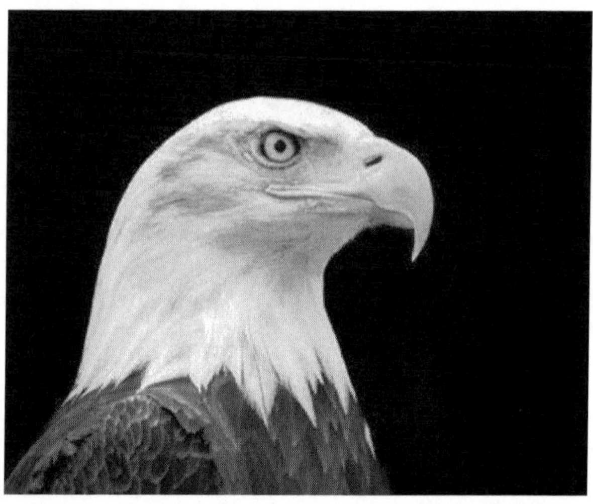

MENTAL PREPARATION

Now that you are physically prepared, you need to be mentally prepared. Many of us will know what being in the zone feels like. It is that place and time when everything seems to work. Where the physical work does not feel as hard as it usually would, where you are hyper-aware of what is going on around you. Where time seems to slow for you so that you have more of it and you are reacting faster than everyone else. For most of us, those moments make you realise what it must feel like to be a true great. If only you could always perform that way.

They are fleeting glimpses of how we could be, but seem as difficult to hold onto as smoke.

"In my mind, I'm always the best. If I walk out on the court and I think the next person is better, I've already lost." -Venus Williams (1980-) Winner of 7 Grand Slam Tennis titles and former World No.1 in Women's Tennis

You might not be able to truly capture those moments, but you can find the zone more consistently and push your performances much closer to that level. As with everything, this takes practice, but it is a process you can learn. There are two major steps to achieving this zone, both processes are similar and once you have perfected one, the other will be relatively easy. The first is to know how to get into the frame of mind you want on the day.

Achieving a Competitive Frame of Mind

You might want to be calm or confident, or you might want to be fired up, the process is the same as long as you are clear on what you feeling you are trying to trigger. What you want to achieve is your particular frame of mind and to be able to call on it whenever you want. The process I am about to describe is based on Neuro Linguistic Programming, or NLP. Different feelings or emotional states can become attached to a particular stimulus. Often, we only notice the negative times that this happens, such as if a loud noise makes you anxious because you previously had a car accident. This is also the case, although we notice it less, with positive events. A particular smell not only brings back the memory of a place that it is attached to for you, but also the feeling that you had when you were there. It is a common technique for training dogs, where the dog gets a treat each time it responds correctly to a particular command and the treat makes the dog happy. Eventually the treat is removed, but the dog retains the feeling of happiness in responding to the command. Although we aren't dogs, the principle is the same. You can train own responses so that you can trigger them at will. It is the building block, the foundation of getting into the zone. I will use the feeling of confidence as an example to demonstrate the process.

"Under pressure, you don't rise to the occasion, you sink to the level of your training. Thats why we train so hard." - Anonymous US Navy Seal.

First you need to practise, so find yourself somewhere quiet and safe where you will be undisturbed. Now, relax and think of a time when you were really confident (or whatever feeling you are trying to evoke). It needs to be some time you really felt this strongly. It could be when you were competing well beneath your level and you were very relaxed and confident in your performance. It might have nothing to do with sport. It could be anything. It is the feeling itself that is important, not the reason that you felt it. Once you remember the time, take yourself back there. Try to remember as much as you can about the time, try and relive it, the run up to the time, the preparation, why you felt so confident. Remind yourself of everything. Who was there and how it felt. Continue remembering until you have the feeling of confidence again, as if you were in that place at that time. Lock onto how it feels, make sure you have it and really feel it. Once you have a strong feeling, you need to anchor it to something. Your anchor needs to be physical. Pinch your thumb and third finger together, squeeze your right earlobe, whatever you want, but something slightly unusual. You will see many professional athletes do something of this nature if you watch them carefully before events.

Once you have your anchor you now need to break it temporarily by doing something else. Walk around, sing a song. Do something to distract yourself for a few minutes. Once you have broken the spell, repeat the process another two or three times, with a break between. Then, repeat the whole thing every few days until you can trigger your anchor at any point without the preparation first and feel confident. You still need to practice to maintain the anchor, but once you have it locked in you just need to use it. You can use it as part of your regular training. If you find it is starting to wane, repeat the process to reset your anchor.

Another option for either creating your anchor or embedding it is when you realise you are in a frame of mind that you would like to replicate in future. Follow the same steps above except that you do not need to visualise or imagine or even remember all the sensory data, you need to become acutely aware of them in your present.

The beauty of this process is that you can have multiple anchors as well. You can be confident in the warm up and then trigger another anchor before the match or event commences.

Where 'The Zone' Is

Before I cover the ways of getting into the zone, first it is worth understanding what an extreme version of being in the zone is, where it occurs and when it occurs accidentally. People think of being in the zone as how I described it earlier in the chapter. But it is more than that; there is a time when you go beyond our usual level and perform 'miracles'. These times are when you have effectively lost the game. It is when you are all but defeated, by all logic there is nothing left to play for.

A recent example was in the 2012 Ryder cup where Europe were trailing 10-6 going into the last day. The USA, with some of the best golfers in the world, only needed to win three matches from twelve, on home soil, on a course specifically set up to suit their skill and with a huge and very partisan crowd. In a similar situation, Liverpool FC left the pitch at half time in the Champion's League final 3-0 behind to a rampant AC Milan in 2005. In the 1999 Rugby World Cup semi-final, France trailed favourites New Zealand 24-10 in the second half of the match. The reports were written, the matches over in everyone's mind except the teams that were losing. Liverpool, pulled all three goals back to draw level in the

first 15 minutes of the second half and went on to win the final on penalties. Europe's golfers stepped up to win match after match in the singles to overturn the deficit and break the hearts of the Americans to win 14 ½ to 13 ½. France went on to completely dominate New Zealand and ran out 43-31 winners.
What happens in these moments where teams or individuals are suddenly transformed? If this can be done as a comeback, what would have happened if they had played like that at the start? They did not suddenly have a major leap in ability. It can only be a change of mindset that prompted the change of result. The reason I chose teams as examples is that, while there are lots of examples of individuals performing the same feats of comebacks, these could be discounted as the opposition 'choking' prompting the collapse, but this is less likely to be the case in team sports. Every single player for AC Milan did not suddenly choke, it was caused by how Liverpool attacked the second half like their very lives depended on it. But if that is the case, why didn't they do that in the first half? This was the European Cup Final, so it cannot be that they weren't motivated.

The answer is that once you are 'certain' of losing, you have nothing more to lose. You can play without fear. You are free from the worry of the outcome and the consequences because it is already over.

On Daniel Coyle's website thetalentcode.com he published the following letter from Jared Mathes, who coaches an U-14 volleyball team in Calgary, Alberta, about finding the 'sweet spot', playing without fear of failure and 'positive errors'.

The one problem I have on my team is having the athletes get over the fear of making a mistake. We do great in practice, but during a tournament, the more "important" the game, the more they regress to predictable, safe playing.

To overcome this, we discussed as a team a few weeks ago that the March 17 tournament would be a "throw-away". We didn't care about the outcome. If players played aggressive they would never be in danger of being subbed off, no matter how many mistakes they made. Everyone bought into the system and was willing to give it a try, except for about half of my parent group. They had a hard time accepting the fact that we were going to let the girls figure it out and let them "go for it" on every ball regardless of the score or the stakes.

As we started the day, we had serves going out and wide. But the team was relaxed and having fun. If they didn't get a great spike in one rally, they tried even harder the next time. They saw that by making positive errors, often the other team would still go for the ball and touch it, giving us a point. As the day progressed, they were becoming more confident. I had athletes who had never attempted jump serving, trying it and succeeding. Our play was getting more aggressive as the day went on and we were constantly winning.

We made it to the semi-finals and all of my doubting parents were congratulating me on the genius of the approach to the tournament. They couldn't believe how well their daughters were playing, and it was just getting better. I cautioned them and reminded them that the focus has to be on the process, not the outcome, and that even if we were in last place, it would still have been a worthy strategy for all the teaching it provided. We played with the most aggression and intelligence we have ever done. We hit from everywhere on the court. It was beautiful to watch.

In the second game of the finals, we were behind 23-19. My athlete who was up to serve was one who had discovered her jump serve throughout the day. In the past, she would have regressed and underhand served because she had no confidence in her overhand serve during a critical time in the match. However, with no fear of messing up, and having the entire bench and coaching staff cheering her on to "go for it!", she let fly an amazing jump serve. Ace! The score is now 23-21 for them. She goes up to do it again. I look over and her mother is covering her eyes. This player has never served 2 jump serves in a row and her mother can't watch. We're all cheering her to go for it. Again, Ace!. Score is 23-22 for them. Confidently, she goes back to serve again. She ends up serving 3 more aces, all off of her newly found jump serve and we win the tournament. The bench is going crazy and the parents are ecstatic. I think her mother suffered a minor heart attack.

The examples of teams coming from behind and the volleyball team playing without fear of failure describes the 'zone' you need to find and get into. Where you can play without fear and like your life depended on it every single game. As I showed earlier, the unique thing about the first examples above was that the teams were so far behind **they had nothing to lose**. The situation was unlikely to get worse. Losing by an even greater margin would not have made the situation worse. It is this that made them free to play the way they did. In the volleyball example, the coach artificially created the same situation.

Getting into 'The Zone'

In 1994 Dan Jansen was the only skater ever to break 36 seconds in the 500m speed skating and he arrived at his final Olympics the favourite to win the gold. However, Jansen had also been favourite in 1988 (failed to make the final in both 500m and 1000m) and in 1992 (finished 4th and 26th in the same events.) In the 500m, his favoured event in which he was world record holder, Jansen finished 8th. His second, back-up event, the 1000m was to be his final ever event in an Olympics.

"I gave up my expectations and thought about the way I wanted to skate. When the gun went off it was that feeling that you dream about as an athlete. I did not hear anybody. I was just so into how relaxed I felt. The first 600m was like I was floating, it was a beautiful feeling."

Dan Jansen describes perfectly what it felt like to be in the zone (Jansen defied expectations and won gold, setting a new world record on the way), so how do you get yourself in the position where you can play or perform that way? To play or compete with freedom and without fear, or as if your life depended on it? In short, how do you get out of your own way and play to your potential? As with everything, it isn't easy and you do have to practice. First you get your frame of mind in the right place with your anchor. Then the steps are similar to the anchoring but it bit more in depth and as with everything it takes practice. It won't work instantly.

Start by remembering a time when you were really in the zone. It might have been for a few moments or a complete event, but pick some time when it really felt good and that everything was working, everything felt easy. It may not have been your best result or necessarily your best performance, just the point that it felt the way you think being in the zone is like.

Once you have it, you need to go there. Do not just think about it and imagine it. Do not just remember it. You have to take yourself back there. Use these prompts to try to fully recreate the experience:

- What did it feel like? "My legs felt like they were pistons, so powerful" or "It felt like I wasn't even touching the ground as I ran". Lock into the feeling and feel it again. Call it up and relive it.

- How did your body feel? I have had sprinters who have run personal bests when they have not been trying. They felt like their body was completely relaxed and loose. How did your body feel?

- What could you see? For some people, their vision narrows, for others they seem to be able to see everything at once. Maybe everything gets clearer for you, much sharper.

- What could you hear, was it nothing or everything?

- What could you smell, was there something specific?

- How was your breathing? Was it long and deep or panting or somewhere in the middle? Through the nose or through the mouth, or both?

- What was your facial expression? Your facial expression is very important. It is an established principle that your facial expression affects how you feel. If you smile, properly, it is difficult to be angry. Your body speaks the mind and vice-versa. In the same way as it is difficult to show a happy face when you are angry, the link also works in the opposite direction. Try it. Smile and see if it makes you feel happier. It is important to remember your facial expression as it is so powerful.

- What was the internal conversation you were having in your head? What were you saying to yourself? Were you encouraging yourself, driving yourself onwards?

Once you have all these things and you know what they are, match them. Not only do you need to relive that moment, you also need to call up all the feelings, the thoughts and the facial expression. You need your body to feel the same as it did, your breathing to be the same. Get your mind in that place where you have nothing to lose, where you can play with freedom (but not recklessness). The way this principle works is very similar to how your facial expression affects your mood, because smiling triggers you to feel happier just as much as feeling happy makes you smile. What you are doing is to find your zone by recreating every single state of your mind and body to match when you were in the zone.

There is no specific trigger or stimulus this time like there was in the earlier technique for calling up a frame of mind. Getting into the zone is a method and takes time, not just to develop the skill, but each time you need to get there. This is not easy and you will need to practise it as part of your training. Try getting in the zone before each training session and each match or competition. To do this you need to find a time and a quiet space to get into that place. It needs to become an integral part of your warm-up routine. Each physical drill is tied to a mental drill and the two build up together so that by the time you race you will be both physically and mentally prepared.

It will be hard at first and you might find it difficult to remember all the different things you are trying to call up from when you were in the zone previously. However, you will start to find that you can get there in some matches. But each time you achieve the feeling of being in the zone, you will find it easier to remember how it felt, what you were thinking and so on because you were more conscious of it.

Summary

Your mind plays a huge part in how you perform and as has been shown, the higher the level you compete, the more important it is.

1. Manage your competition mental state by practising how you want to feel and anchoring the feeling to a physical action so you call up this mental state at any time.

2. Practice getting into the zone so you can play every game at the peak of your performance level.

CHAPTER 14

TURNING YOUR WEAKNESSES INTO STRENGTHS

This chapter is based on a number of different theories, mostly from outside of sport. It is important that I give credit to others for the original work but I will only cover them in sufficient detail for you to understand them, leaving out the bits that aren't applicable to sport. You only need to understand how to use what is important from them, so I have kept the background information brief to get into the 'how-to' quickly.

The Pareto Principle (mostly known as the 80/20 rule)

In the early part of the last century an Italian economist called Vilfredo Pareto observed that 20% of the pea pods in his garden contained 80% of the peas. Taking his study further, he found that 20% of the people in Italy owned 80% of the land. This phenomenon of a small portion of the whole having a disproportional impact became known as the Pareto principle or the 80/20 rule and has become very well used as a rule of thumb. Although not intended to be exact numbers, as a general rule for the distribution of anything 80% of the results come from 20% of the factors. So for a business, 80% of the sales will come from 20% of their customers. It won't be exact, but you can gauge quickly where the 20% is and you can act on the information without doing a great deal of analysis.

What does the Pareto Principle mean to you?

As an athlete, in any sport, there will be things that you work on and things that you do not. Unless you are already elite (in which case, congratulations) you will have limited time in which to train. The remainder of your time will be taken up by your other commitments, probably studies, possibly work, maybe both, plus other commitments and anything else you are either unable or unprepared to sacrifice. So training time is precious and it is very important to get the absolute greatest effect from each session. So how do you, or your coach, decide what to work on?

"Things which matter most must never be at the mercy of things which matter least." - Johann Wolfgang von Goethe (1749-1832) German writer and politician.

So you work on your weaknesses, right? Turn them into strengths and everything will be fine, which is what this chapter is about.

Yes.

And no.

Yes, you want to work on your weaknesses because that's where the gains are. But you will have more than one weakness and we have already established that you have limited time to train. You cannot only work on your weaknesses because you need to maintain everything else, so your time within your training is limited. So you now need to decide which weakness to target, but how?

Firstly you have to realise that your biggest weakness is not where you necessarily think it is. Let's use a simple example and go back to our 100m sprinter. If his maximum speed is not as good as his nearest rival then you would think that that is probably the most important factor for a 100m runner. Yet, the period of a 100m race that is run at maximum speed is only around 18%. The acceleration phase of the race is a staggering 64%. If our athlete has a weakness here, it will have a much bigger impact on his/her performance than their top speed. It may not be 80% but it is close enough. For some simple maths, a 5% improvement in the acceleration will be a lot more effective than a 5% improvement in top speed on the overall time of the race. It will probably be no more or less difficult to achieve but the result is much greater. Where will you put your training time?

"Don't run away from a challenge. Instead run toward it cause the only way to escape fear is to trample it beneath your feet" – Nadia Comaneci (1961-) Five-time Olympic gold medal winning gymnast and the first gymnast to score a perfect 10 in an Olympic event.

You do not need to remember that you are using the Pareto Principle, you do not need to call it the 80/20 rule, you just need put your effort where it has most effect, not try to hit everything at once. You do not really need to use a great deal of analysis. Either you or your coach just needs to recognise where you are losing most or where your main weaknesses are.

The Theory of Constraints

There is a book called The Goal written by Eli Goldratt, whom I introduced in Chapter 6, that is number 10 in Time magazine's 25 Most Influential Business Management Books of all time. Considering that the business management book industry is huge, this is an amazing feat. The book is written as a novel and the theories in the book aren't laid bare, they are part of the story and the book teaches you the theory in what is called a Socratic method. The characters in the book, and the reader, are left to work out the problems for themselves with guidance, rather than have them spelled out in clear terms. A little bit like how coaches help athletes to learn rather than tell them where they are going wrong.

The book is about managing a manufacturing plant and the problems its manager has at the factory and at home. But why would a business book which is a story about manufacturing have any relevance to an athlete? The key is in understanding who Goldratt is. He wasn't a management guru, a manufacturing executive, a consultant or a business theorist. He was, and still is, a physicist. Sport is about physics. Newton's laws of motion are the foundation of every sport. Now Goldratt, a physicist, has written a method of understanding how to overcome weakness. While it isn't based on Newton's Laws, it is based on physics. It is based on the principle of levers, the same principle that biomechanics is based on – amplifying an input force to create a greater output force. In other words, the book is about finding the point of greatest leverage. It would be easy to state that Goldratt unwittingly wrote about sport, but the Theory of Constraints has been applied to many different applications in many industries and disciplines. Having met Eli Goldratt, I'm sure he would say it is applicable to anything that you are aiming to improve. The Theory is stunning in its simplicity but that makes it more powerful not less.

There are some elements of the theory that are irrelevant to us, but what is key is the Process of Ongoing Improvement (POOGI), or more usually The Five Steps:

1. Identify the Constraint
2. Exploit the Constraint
3. Subordinate everything else to the Constraint
4. Elevate the constraint
5. Return to step 1 if you have a new constraint

How the Five Steps work for Sport

Identify the Constraint

This is where the Pareto Principle comes in. What weakness is holding you back the most? What is having the greatest effect on your improvement? This will often be a certain part of your performance, but not always. It might be a mental toughness issue, where you cannot perform in important competitions due to nerves. It might be a nutrition or hydration issue. It might even be access to a place to train, or lack of opportunity to train.

Exploit the constraint.

This is about how to get the most out of what you have. If you are a soccer player and your constraint is your fitness how do you get the most out of it? You can play a position that requires a lower level of fitness, playing centre back rather than centre midfield for example, or your style of play may conserve energy and utilise other skills instead. Your constraint may be in facilities. If you are a cricket player who trains in an indoor sports hall and it's only available for 1 hour a week, then I have seen teams turn up, do their warm ups and some fitness work for the first 15 or 20 minutes, then practice for the remainder. That is not exploiting the constraint. You do not need to warm up in the sports hall; you can do it anywhere, outside waiting to go in. You can do fitness work anywhere and it does not even have to be the same day. You have an hour to practice in the indoor facility so you must exploit that to the maximum. If it is a performance constraint, such as a golfer who has not got a good Putt, then you have to exploit what you have. If you can only sink from 4 foot or less, then get yourself in a position to sink from 4 foot or less. Do not try to sink putts from 16 foot and end up still more than 4 foot from the pin. Make the most of what you have.

Subordinate everything else to the constraint.

This is about decision making. If there is a choice to be made then you choose the option that allows you to make the most of your constraint. Team GB Middle Distance runner Mo Farah CBE won two Olympic Golds in 2012 by running to his constraints. Farah ran both races tactically that not only played to his strengths, but limited the opportunities for his competitors to exploit his weakness. It is testament to the Olympic Champion that he succeeded in doing this and managed such a long race to his own constraints leaving himself in the position where his absolute strength of his finish was still available at the end. A 400m race is shorter but quite similar. In its simplest form, an athlete must run a lap as fast as he or she can, but as the 400m is such a long sprint there are different ways of achieving it. The athlete runs the first 250m at a high pace and then maintains that pace as best they can for the final 150m. The reality is a bit more complicated than this over-simplification, but generally this is correct and serves our purpose. The big question for the sprinter is how fast to run the first section. Leaving tactics aside, if you are a sprinter who is fast over the short sprints, your constraint will be how fast your speed drops off in the final stage. If you are a longer sprinter, then you may not have the top end speed, but you can hold a slightly lower speed than the short sprinter for longer. At the end of the race, the one who has exploited their constraint the best will win, not the one who has exploited their strength. Women's World 400m champion Christine Ohuruogu MBE runs a very slow (relative to her competition) first 250m but a very fast last 150m. Her outright speed is a constraint but her speed-endurance wins championships.

Elevate the Constraint.

In one sense, if the constraint is not you, then this means find a way to get the more of what you need. So if your constraint is that your team does not play or train enough, join another team that does, or join a team that plays and trains at different times as well as your current team. Now you have twice as much playing and practice time. If it is facilities, then find one that costs the same (if this is limiting you) but where you might get more time for the same money. It also means being creative. Sprint teams need to do speed work in the winter but cold weather is notorious for causing injuries at high intensities. Some teams I know of that have no indoor facility train in long corridors in schools when the school is closed. You may have to think outside the box a little.

If this is about your performance though, it simply means get better at your weakness. Your weaknesses are usually the things you like practising the least. You will prefer to do the stuff you are good at. These will be the things you dread coming up at training. But you have already identified that this is where the gains are. This 20% of your event will get you 80% of your performance gains, so it is definitely worth the grind. If that is not enough to motivate you, then try and re-evaluate why you hate it so much, why it is a weakness. Maybe everyone hates it and you just didn't realise. Sir Bradley Wiggins, Tour de France and many time Olympic medallist, said "You can't justify saying for the rest of your career 'Well, actually, you know what? I'm not that good at climbing'. If that's the case you have to work on climbing. The art is in working on your weaknesses without losing what you're good at."

When I was a football coach and player, everyone hated fitness work. There was a limited amount of fitness required to be a footballer and most people did enough (or so everyone told themselves) and no more. Often, playing football itself was seen to be sufficient. Fitness work was the stuff you did for a couple of weeks in pre-season. Other than that it wasn't a good use of time. However, players with a proper level of fitness that could cover the ground were faster and could be still playing at a high level at the last period of the game and even into extra time. They stood out. In almost all cases, these players participated in another sport that led to their fitness level. They were runners, sprinters, gymnasts, swimmers. It was very rare for them to be doing this just for football, but still the other players would not recognise how much better this made them. If fitness is your constraint, it does not matter whether you like it or not, you are pursuing a dream.

Another way to approach your constraint is to change the way you look at it. As a cyclist, I was too big to enjoy hills. I stuck to time trials as these were flatter. Then I read that Sir Bradley Wiggins who was also a time triallist and track cyclist just approached hills like a time trial. Instead of trying to dance up the hill like his rival Alberto Contador, he just locked in to a time trial effort and went up the hill, same effort level all the way up no matter the gradient of the hill. That worked for me, I stopped looking at hills the same way and they didn't bother me anymore.

If all else fails and you hate training to overcome your weakness (your constraint), then there is one last resort you can take. Start saying you love that aspect of your training. Read that again and no, you didn't misread it. It is a stupid thing to say, right? The Olympic speed skater from the US, Dan Jansen who I introduced in the last chapter, seemed destined to be the best speed skater of a generation without ever winning an Olympic medal. It is fair to say that he 'failed' to win medals in previous Olympics because he was hot favourite in 1984, 88 and 1992. In an interview on TV, he said that before his final Olympics in 1994 Jansen tried to address his least favourite event, the 1000m. "First of all, every day, I wrote in my diary, 'I love the 1000m', but I also would write little notes and post them up around the house, on the refrigerator, the bathroom mirror and everywhere so I would walk round and see 'I love the 1000m'. But strangely enough that combined with other things we did. I'll never forget the day that I literally thought to myself 'I can't wait for the 1000m and I never said that before, never thought that before". Jansen went onto win the 1000m Olympic Gold and break the World Record in the process.

Just saying you love the really tough workouts that leave everyone on the floor or vomiting does not seem like enough to overcome your dislike of them. And yet it does work. Not always, but often enough that it is worth trying. This seems overly simple, so I think it is worth understanding the theory. This is based on the pleasure/pain principle which in Freudian psychology is the psychoanalytical concept describing people seeking pleasure and avoiding suffering (pain) in order to satisfy biological and psychological needs.

There are two elements to this. First is that what you **believe** will bring pleasure or pain may be different from the reality and certainly different in the intensity that you expect. That training session isn't ever as bad as you expect it to be. The second is that often your energy gets sapped by your expectation. Rather than worrying about how you will feel, focus on the present, how you feel now. In Chapter 5, I mentioned a saying I have: "The gate's not locked." You have a choice. You don't have to do the hard stuff, you choose to do it. That distinction is very important psychologically.

So for the workouts you find really tough say out loud, to your training mates, that you enjoy them. See what their reaction is. See what your reaction is. Say it like you mean it. You will start to believe it. Focus on the now rather than how it will feel at the end. It is a "virtuous circle". By saying it you will start to believe it because you are changing your expectation and, as I stated earlier, your expectation is usually worse than reality. By doing it you will improve and as you improve it will get easier. You will hate it less and start to believe what you say. On top of that you will realise that a lot of your teammates will give you respect for loving the tough stuff. You'll get a reputation for being a hard worker. You will enjoy your reputation and it will add to your change in approach to the element you hate. Suddenly you will realise it is no longer your biggest weakness.

Return to step 1 if you have a new constraint.

This five step process is also known as the Process of **ongoing** improvement. Once your constraint is not a constraint anymore, your weakness is no longer a weakness, then you need to find your next one and keep going until you eventually retire. Your weakness eventually will stop being proper weaknesses in the strictest sense. If you are in the Olympic Final then the amount of "weaknesses" you have will be very limited, but you will still have constraints that might prevent you from winning. Even in this case, the process is the same.

Summary

If you apply both of these theories to identify and overcome your weaknesses you will see significant improvements. Use the 80/20 rule to prioritise where you are going to get the most gain and then use the five focussing steps to exploit your constraint to the maximum effect until you have another constraint.

1. Identify your constraint (80/20 rule)
2. Exploit your constraint
3. Subordinate everything else to your constraint
4. Elevate your constraint
5. Return to step 1 if you have a new constraint

CHAPTER 15

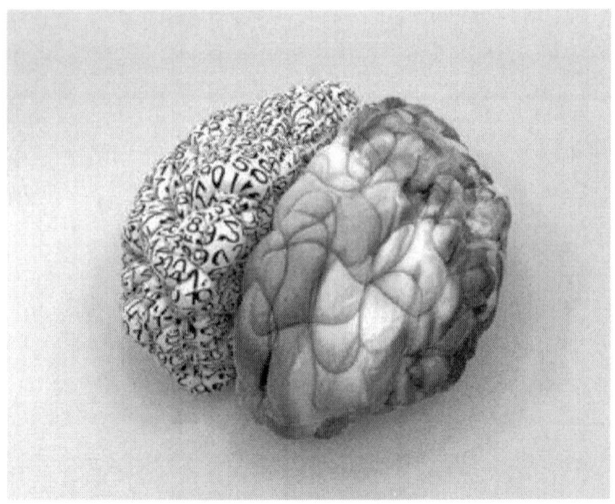

A WINNING MINDSET

As a coach, I used to be able to tell which athletes were going to be really good. Whether it was football or track and field, I could tell. There was something about them but it wasn't the obvious signs. Yes, of course they were athletic in the true sense of the word. They had great balance and movement. They were the kinds of kids who would be good at any sport. Usually. Not always. Sometimes, they weren't that kid, they were a little awkward and graceless. But there was something that made them stand out.

It was usually in their attitude. Not just how they approached me. It was how they approached the sport. For one thing, they played without fear. They 'had a go'. If I threw them into a game, they played. It didn't matter how good the other kids were, or that they were struggling. They didn't shy away from the challenge. If they joined the sprint group at the athletics club and I started them off in a warm up, the drills can be quite difficult, new movement patterns that they haven't done before. But they would just stand next to someone and copy them. Again, they would 'have a go'.

The other thing was that you could see them learn. You could see their brain working when a coach spoke. Processing the information. Turning it over in their head. Trying this new information out in their mind. Sometimes they would close their eyes, visualising a move they've never done before. Or making small movements to try to prepare themselves for what they would be about to do.

The other thing was that they were trying to be as good, or better, than everyone else. It wasn't that they were trying to be top dog. Far from it. These were the kids that came to me because they were too good for wherever they had come from and weren't learning anything there. They didn't want to be top dog, they wanted to be somewhere that they had to strive to be. It was never expressed that way of course, but it is what I saw.

Eventually, I realised that I was wrong. I realised that those people who think they could talent-spot this way (and many people do - although they might describe it differently), and I was among them, were mistaken. I was lucky in that I would never filter anyone out to focus on the 'talented' ones, so my mistake didn't negatively affect anyone too badly.

My mistake wasn't with the kids that seemed to be 'talented', although I'm sure I hindered some of them and allowed them to drift from the development path they were on. It was with everyone else. What I didn't realise was that the only difference between these so-called 'talented' kids was in their mindset. They had a growth mindset where others had a fixed mindset. Until I wrote this book, I didn't understand this for what it was and that their mindset could be developed into a growth mindset by how I spoke to them, how their parents spoke to them and what was said. Even when I wrote the book, it was a small, but important, part of a chapter.

This chapter is based on a series of articles I wrote of Jimson Lee at speedendurance.com. He asked me to write something on how to deal with poor performance and I knew the subject was too big to write in one short article. Even then, once I'd written the articles, it was immediately obvious to me that I wanted to write more.

The growth mindset is the biggest performance enhancer there is. Will a growth mindset guarantee success? No. There are too many other factors involved. But without it will success be all but impossible? More than likely. And success in anything is difficult enough as it is.

This chapter will describe the mindset, how to use it as an athlete, as a coach and as a parent/guardian.

Fixed and Growth Mindset

To understand the importance of a person's mindset and the profound effect it can have, it is worth taking some time to understand the background. As Jennifer Aniston would say, "here comes the science bit."

Professor Carol Dweck PhD is a world-renowned Stanford University psychologist who has written a number of articles and books. She has been interested in what motivates people since she was 15 years old and during a study of what makes people successful, she made the breakthrough which led to her book 'Mindset: The New Psychology of Success'. During the study, involving High School Fifth-Graders, the 400 students were given an easy IQ test. They were randomly selected into two groups and each group were given simple but specific praise. Group 1 were told "Wow, you got [x many] right. That's a really good score. You must be smart at this". Group 2 were told "Wow, you got [x many] right. That's a really good score. You must have worked really hard". Nothing more.

They were then offered another task but had two options.

They could take a harder test with the opportunity to learn and grow.

They could take a similar test, which played to their strengths and they were certain to do well.

From Group 1 (The "smart" group) 67% chose to take Option 2, the easy task. From Group 2 (workers), 97% chose the harder task.

The smart group had been pushed into a fixed mindset, rejecting a challenging new task that they could learn from because they did not want to do anything that would expose flaws or damage their perception of their talent. Success in the test meant they were intelligent, because that is what they had been told. Therefore anything less than success, in a very simple logical equation, meant they were somehow lacking. The work group on the other hand wanted the task they could learn from. They did not see greater difficulty as a reflection of their intellect, they simply thought they had to put in more effort.

Later, both groups were given a tough, almost impossible, test. Group 2 worked harder, for longer and enjoyed the test. Group 1 got frustrated and gave up early. In the first test, both groups enjoyed the test because it was within their capability. The worker group also enjoyed the challenge of the second test, but in stark contrast, the smart group no longer had any fun.

So far, so strange. But the test didn't stop there. The kids were then asked to write a letter to their peers about the tests and include their test scores in the letter. Forty percent of the kids from the "smart" group, the ones praised for their ability, lied about their scores and inflated them to look more successful.

Then, a third test was set at exactly the same difficulty (easy) as the very first one. Group 1, the "smart" group, did worse than on their first test and reduced overall performance by 20%. Group 2 did better than the first test and improved performance by 30%. This is a 50% performance swing from a single sentence of praise!

"You must be smart at this" versus "You must have worked really hard".

The implications of this intervention could not be more profound, for parents, teachers, coaches and athletes.

You can quickly see why this discovery led Dweck down the road of researching this model further. The model she settled on was that people have one of two 'mindsets'. (I apologise for the gross oversimplification of Dweck's work. Read the book, the Amazon link is here). They will either have a "fixed" or a "growth" mindset. Even the original study that prompted this one, on lab animals, is quite profound. Even lab animals were found to exhibit "learned helplessness" where they didn't do something they were capable of because they had given up from repeated failure.

For a long time (and in a lot of cases, this is still present now), people believed that a "cure" for helplessness and failure was a string of successes. Dweck didn't believe this to be the case. She felt that most important element lay in people's belief of why they had failed. The difference in response, helplessness or a determination to master new things, was caused by either a belief in a lack of ability, or that they hadn't tried hard enough respectively. It is easy to see how these beliefs would drive the responses that Dweck observed.

In a different study, Dweck was observing children completing a task that was too difficult for them to see how they attributed failure. She was surprised to find that some children didn't see the difficulty as a failure at all. Her collaborator on the study, Carol Diener puts it this way: "Failure is information—we label it failure, but it's more like, 'This didn't work, I'm a problem solver, and I'll try something else.'" During one unforgettable moment, one boy—something of a poster child for the mastery-oriented type—faced his first stumper by pulling up his chair, rubbing his hands together, smacking his lips and announcing, "I love a challenge."

The Characteristics of a Fixed Mindset Individual

People are born 'Gifted'

People have 'natural talents'

Traits are set in stone

Intelligence is a fixed trait

They have a need to look smart at all costs,

Tasks should come naturally

They avoid challenging learning tasks

They hide mistakes and difficulties

In the face of failure they would reduce their effort or give up, become defensive, act up, act bored.

Characteristics of a Growth mindset

Success comes from effort

Success comes from hard work

Success comes from practice

Intelligence can be improved

Setbacks are a natural form of learning

Learn at all costs,

Work hard, effort is key

Capitalise on mistakes and confront deficiencies

In the face of a setback they would work harder

They are resilient in the face of difficulties

The Power of Praise

We are all told to praise our kids, or the athletes we coach. "Give them lots of praise!" we're told. Enable them. Give them confidence and they will do well. It seems that this advice is fundamentally lacking and that the wrong kind of praise is not only incorrect, it is actually destructive. All the characteristics listed above of the two mindsets will be evident in people around you. Your kids, your peers, the athletes you coach. If they are driven by medals, or scoring goals, or being first, strongest or whatever, it will seem on the surface that they are driven to be a winner. That's what we think we need, someone who is fiercely competitive like athlete 'x' or player 'y'. They play to win.

But this could not be more wrong and is rarely a feature of the elite athletes who are successful Obviously, they are fiercely competitive and are playing to win, but more than that, they are playing to test themselves, playing to learn, to develop. Why is this? It is because we almost always see them when they are already elite, but don't consider how they got there. If you think about people that you know that have seemed like they would definitely 'make it' because they were so talented - everyone says so - but then don't. There are always reasons, excuses, but it is the very certainty of their 'talent' that often leads to their failure. The reality is that these people have been programmed into a fixed mindset. They believe in their own talent. Natural talent does not need effort, it does not need to be trained like regular people - the less endowed - and it does not need help.

That's okay, until you move up to a new standard, where you aren't the best anymore. You go to an academy, or an international race. Suddenly not only are you being measured against equals, you are probably being measured against people better than you. A fixed mindset person with their 'innate' talent will not only dislike the failure, they will simply be unable to understand it and they will go to pieces.

The growth mindset on the other hand is often the person who has had to always work, or be lucky enough that they have developed a growth mindset through circumstances. They will see the new circumstances as a new challenge, something that will help them. Often, they will actively seek it out for this reason.

How to Create a Growth Mindset

As coaches or parents, our aim is to create better athletes and it is clear from the mindset model that all athletes need a growth mindset.

How to give praise

We all want to support our athletes and give them lots of praise because we believe this is encouraging. In a short term view, this is correct. However, praise can actually do more harm than good if done incorrectly as we saw in Chapter 2. So how do you give appropriate praise that ensures athletes have no fear of failure and encourage an improvement philosophy?

First, praise should not be biased to their results. Praise must focus on effort and the process that they are adopting. Obviously, progress is measured by results, but this needs to be managed carefully. The messages here are critical to development. All coaches know that a kid who wins races with sheer brute force and no technique will eventually get beaten by a superior technique as the athletes develop and then they will never recover the gap. We know this, so it is clear that the end does not justify the means. I'm sure all of us have explained and accepted a dip in performance with an athlete while we correct something for a longer term gain. There is no difference in what I am proposing here. The process is key, not the result. The result will inevitably follow.

Praising results or talent can turn athletes off to improving. They will choose easier tasks to reinforce the label they are given. Beating people and coming first becomes more important to them than improvement and growth. This was a revelation for me and yet with hindsight I can see where it has happened. I have had athletes that are so ingrained in results that they have chosen lower level competitions over national level ones just because they wouldn't win the higher competition. Or others who have simply not entered the high level competition that they qualified for because they knew they couldn't win. The experience and learning opportunity meant nothing to them.

As Dweck says "If you want to demonstrate something over and over, it feels like something static that lives inside of you—whereas if you want to increase your ability, it feels dynamic and malleable"

In Dweck's study, praising results is a retrograde capability which in our case would result in a lowering of performance. When returning from a hard race that involves some failure, back to an easier race that would previously have been successful, the result is often a further failure. Fear of failure then creates failure.

If the child hears that you think they are brilliant and talented they start to believe that is why you admire or are proud of them. "I better not do anything to disprove your evaluation." As a result they enter a fixed mindset and they play it safe in future and limit the growth of their talent.

In an article in the Stanford Magazine (March/April 2007) called The Effort Effect, the manager of the youth academy of UK football team Blackburn Rovers, Tony Faulkner, went to Dweck for help.

Faulkner knew that his most talented individuals disdained serious training. British soccer culture lives on the belief that star players are born, not made. If you are told that you have immense talent, what's the point of practice? If anything, training hard would tell you and others that you're merely good, not great. The Rovers players didn't think they lacked what it took to succeed. Quite the opposite: they thought their talent was enough. The whole culture of football, not just the individuals or even the club, was one of a fixed mindset.

As coaches and parents we must focus on the strategies they use and encourage them to stretch themselves into taking on hard tasks or praising the intense practise they are doing. Those are the kinds of things that say to a child or athlete that it is about the process of growth. If I don't take on hard things and stick to them, I'm not going to grow and the coach is not going to praise me.

The most important word in the coach or parent's dictionary.

Use the word 'YET'

Failure is binary. Win/Lose. Success/Failure. Yes/No.

In contrast, "Not yct" means you haven't finished. If your athlete makes a binary statement, then add the word YET to it.

I'm not good at………{add yet}

I can't do ……..{add yet}

I tried …………but it didn't work {add yet}

Taking it further

Once this mindset is embedded for you, it needs to be extended further. First, it is not enough for you to use that language with an athlete with a fixed mindset to change them. You must do it with all your athletes. Further, you must do it when you talk about other athletes. Praise the way they train, how hard they work and link their performance to that. Whether it is talking about someone else in the group or Kirani James, the language has to be consistent. Secondly, as important as we coaches are, we are rarely the most important person in the athlete's life. Parents need to adopt the same language and methods of praise. Parents of athletes that aren't at the top of their sport, or their event do this naturally. If they aren't winning then what else is there? They have to praise the effort. Often kids who achieve brilliant results early and receive amazing plaudits and praise for how talented they are, will fade away later. The average kids suddenly start to break through and put in high performances. The link is obvious.

In a further Standford Magazine Article called What Do We Tell the Kids, Dweck cited these examples.

Listen to what you say to your kids, with an ear toward the messages you're sending about mind-set.

Instead of praising children's intelligence or talent, focus on the processes they used.

Example: "That homework was so long and involved. I really admire the way you concentrated and finished it."

Example: "That picture has so many beautiful colours. Tell me about them."

Example: "You put so much thought into that essay. It really makes me think about Shakespeare in a new way."

When your child messes up, give constructive criticism—feedback that helps the child understand how to fix the problem, rather than labelling or excusing the child.

Pay attention to the goals you set for your children; having innate talent is not a goal, but expanding skills and knowledge is.

Don't worry about praising your children for their inherent goodness, though. It's important for children to learn they're basically good and that their parents love them unconditionally, Dweck says. "The problem arises when parents praise children in a way that makes them feel that they're good and love-worthy only when they behave in particular ways that please the parents."

Listen for the messages in the following examples:

"You learned that so quickly! You're so smart!"

"Look at that drawing. Martha, is he the next Picasso or what?"

"You're so brilliant, you got an A without even studying!"

If you're like most parents, you hear these as supportive, esteem-boosting messages. But listen more closely. See if you can hear another message. It's the ones that children hear:

"If I don't learn something quickly, I'm not smart."

"I shouldn't try drawing anything hard or they'll see I'm no Picasso."

"I'd better quit studying or they won't think I'm brilliant."

Dealing with poor performance

With a growth mindset approach, each race or competition is an opportunity for growth, an opportunity to learn. The athlete will be more focused on competing against people better than them, so "poor" performances will not be about winning or losing. They will only be about failing to execute effectively. However, with a growth mindset the emphasis is on learning and therefore, unless the athlete fails to learn from their experience, whether they were unable to execute effectively or not, there can be no failure. Simply, if your objective is to learn something from the event, then there can be no binary success or failure.

You can see that once you have managed to adopt this mindset (as a coach and with your athlete), simply focusing on the learning points will be a sufficient way to manage poor performance.

Adopting a Growth Mindset

Twelve-year old Jane is on her way to her first club athletics meet. She is lanky, flexible, and "athletic", she loves athletics and everyone feels she is just right for it. Although a little nervous about competing everyone, herself included, felt confident she'd do well. She could already picture herself with her medals.

Jane did well in the events she competed in but was beaten by stronger, more experienced athletes. This had never happened to her in school sports. In each event, she did well, but not enough to win. By the end of the competition, Jane was distraught.

If you were Jane's parents or coach, what should you tell her? These are the typical responses and the analysis of them in fixed and growth mindset terms.

Tell Jane you thought she was the best.

She clearly was not the best, athletics is a brutally honest sport that has no subjectivity. The tape or the clocks don't lie – you know it, and she does too. This offers her no ideas for how to recover or how to improve.

Reassure her that athletics is not that important in the grand scheme of things.

This teaches Jane to devalue something if she doesn't do well in it right away. This is not a message you want her to take away from this experience.

Tell her how good she is and that she will win next time.

This is a very dangerous message in mindset terms. Does ability automatically take you where you want to go? If she didn't win at this meet, why should she win at the next one?

Tell her she didn't deserve to win.

This seems hardhearted under the circumstances and of course you wouldn't say it exactly that way, but be careful how you dress it up. But, if you have a growth mindset and you want your child or athlete to adopt the same, then you need to face the realities.

For all the work we put in as coaches in training and developing the athlete or as parents in raising our children, if they are unable to perform when it counts or to grow and improve because they are holding themselves back mentally, we are merely spinning our wheels.

Whether you completely agree with Dweck's Mindset model or not, ask yourself this question. It could be correct, so if I implemented it anyway, what is the downside?

Get Daniel Coyle's term "Positive Errors" or Eric Thomas' "Fail Forward" into your vocabulary and unleash your fearless athletes on this world!

Failing Forward

In Chapter 14, I devote a whole chapter to why failure is good. It is critical that you develop this growth mindset because to be able to fail and see failure as a positive step is crucial to your development as an athlete.

"The opposite to success is not failure. It is mediocrity. Failure is simply part of the process of success" – Randy Gage

"Only the weak attempts to accomplish what he knows he can already achieve" – Stella Juarez

The whole point of training is to get better, to learn new things and to push yourself. There are times when it is appropriate to be the best, but these are when a competition matters, when it is important to be noticed. What will get you there is failure, being second best.

Be clear though, this does not mean that you should accept failure, quite the opposite in fact. You must put yourself in a position where you are a long way from being the best and then do everything you can possibly do to become the best. If you get there, find another situation where you are no longer the best and start the process again.

This means putting yourself into competitions where you are going to get beat, or putting yourself in a training group or age group that is better than you are right now.

What the mindset feels like

If you have a fixed mindset, the section above will not work for you. If you look at all the characteristics of a fixed mindset described earlier, then you will experience all of these.

Here are some examples of the type of thought processes that are inherent to the two mindsets:

When do you feel smart?

Fixed mindset:

— "When I don't make any mistakes."

— "It's when I finish first and it's perfect."

— "When something is easy for me and others can't do it."

Growth mindset:

— "When it's really hard, and I try hard, and I can do something I couldn't before."

— "When I work on something a long time and finally figure it out."

This is where your journey starts. Where do you need to be that will allow yourself to join that group, or enter that competition, to release your comfort blanket? It can only be a growth mindset.

Start with your objectives:

What do I want out of this competition?

What do I want to learn?
How am I going to get that from this event?

Your objective is to have a learning outcome, something you can take away. If that is your objective, then as long as you learn what you came to learn, then you have been successful. If you are testing yourself against people that are better than you, then you can start to look at where they are better and start to work on those to narrow the gap. It is then the gap that is your measure of progress, not a binary win/lose outcome.

Growth-mindset thinking results in:

— A love for learning and self-improvement.

— A desire to be challenged.

— A willingness to work for positive results.

— A belief that you can control the outcomes in your life with effort and practice.

—The ability to learn from mistakes and failures.

— Emotional resilience.

So focus on the process. If it is a tough session, how long can you match that other person? Then, can you hang in one more rep next time? If you're 6 seconds behind in this race, can you get to 5? Then 4?

What if it still goes wrong?

Sometimes though, you'll make your plans and you'll be focused on your learning outcomes, on the process of how you are doing your race, not the result, and the wheels will still fall off and it will all go awry.

In that case, here is a simple mechanism for dealing with it.

Take a piece of paper and write on it everything that contributed to your performance not being as you expected. Include everything you can think of. It might not just be about what you did; it can and should include what other people did.

Take the list and assign an A and a B to every item. Assign an A if that item is within your control (be careful here to make sure you are taking responsibility appropriately. If you could or should have done something different that would have led to a better performance, that is an A, even if it meant setting off earlier to avoid traffic). The B's are for the things that you could not have controlled; your competitors performance, the organisers and so on.

Now write these onto two separate pieces of paper, one for the A's and one for the B's. Do a last check that the B's couldn't be controlled and then screw that list up and throw it away. If you could have no influence on them, then there is no point worrying about them, so throw it away and forget about them. Burn it if it makes you feel better, as long as you are releasing yourself from all the Bs.

Now you have a list of the things (the A list) that you could have done better or controlled more and you can deal with each item. Decide what you are going to do differently next time, then implement your actions and start to prepare for the next time you compete.

You have learned from the experience you just had and grown with it. Until you become elite, the consequences of that performance aren't terminal and even then, they are only temporarily terminal. The main target for all athletes is improvement and that should override all other considerations.

But consider this scenario from Mindset.com on The Mindset of Athletes:

So great is the belief in natural talent, that many scouts and coaches search only for naturals, and teams will vie with each other to pay exorbitant amounts to recruit them. Billy Beane was a natural. Everyone agreed he was the next Babe Ruth. But Billy Beane lacked one thing. The mindset of a champion.

By the time Beane was a sophomore in high school, he was the highest scorer on the basketball team, the quarterback of the football team, and the best hitter on the baseball team, batting .500 in one of the toughest leagues in the country. His talent was real enough.

But the minute things went wrong, Beane searched for something to break. "It wasn't merely that he didn't like to fail; it was as if he didn't know how to fail."

As he moved up in baseball from the minor leagues to the major leagues, things got worse and worse. Each at-bat became a nightmare, another opportunity for humiliation, and with every botched at-bat, he went to pieces. As one scout said, "Billy was of the opinion that he should never make an out." Sound familiar?

Did Beane try to fix his problems in constructive ways? No, of course not, because this is a story of the fixed mindset. Natural talent should not need effort. Effort is for the others, the less endowed. Natural talent does not ask for help. It is an admission of weakness. In short, the natural does not analyze his deficiencies and coach or practice them away. The very idea of deficiencies is terrifying.

Being so imbued with the fixed mindset, Beane was trapped. Trapped by his huge talent. Beane the player never recovered from the fixed mindset.

Fear of failure, not knowing how to fail or an over-reaction to failure will cripple you in sporting terms.

Impact of fixed and growth mindsets

Labelling people as smart, clever or talented (or derivations of these) creates an expectation in them. Therefore, some types of praise trigger worse performance. People will do things to "prove" the label they have been given, creating a fixed mindset. This creates insecurity so, when something doesn't come naturally, it means they are not capable and look wanting.

People then avoid the things that they need to do to get better in order to protect the 'special' label they have been given.

When the message is changed to rewarding effort, then people react differently and adopt a growth mindset. Credit needs to go to effort and time on task, but these messages have to be changed across the board both to the people, yourself and when discussing others. There is little use attempting to adopt a growth mindset if you consider others ‘naturally’ talented. Is Tiger Woods successful because of natural talent or because he has been working to improve his golf since he was 2 years old?

Summary

The impact of mindset, and the simple language or semantics we use for praise, have an incredibly profound effect on sports development. As a general rule of thumb, kids who develop a growth mindset have more chance of being successful in the long term, both in sports and in life, than those with a fixed mindset. This isn’t exclusively true, but it is generally true.

In other words, you are seriously inhibiting either your own, or your charge’s potential by adopting or allowing a fixed mindset.

Develop a growth mindset

Modify your language in terms of praise, of yourself and of others.

Focus on the learning and the challenge, not the outcome or the achievement

CHAPTER 16

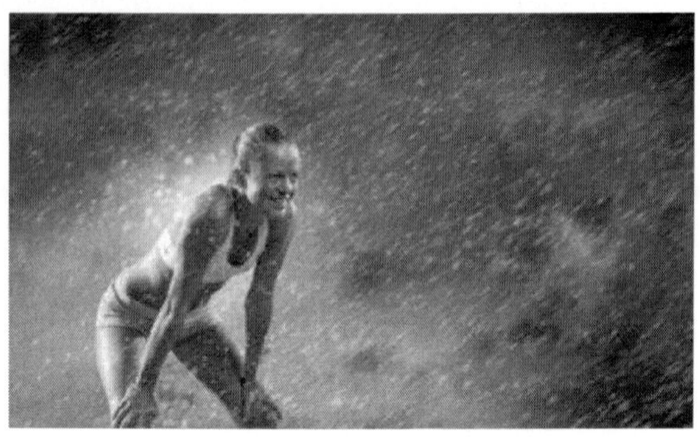

SETTING YOURSELF UP TO FAIL

"The opposite to success is not failure. It is mediocrity. Failure is simply part of the process of success" – Randy Gage (present) US Motivational Speaker and Author

This is a very important principle. Unless you are actually THE number one, being the number one is a bad thing. That may seem incorrect, but what it means is that unless you are at the top of your sport, being the top of your training group or your team or even your area is not a good thing for your progress. Being a big fish in a little pond will not push you to better things. So often, people reach the top of their own little hill and then fade away. This is especially true in the developing years. Some of this can be explained by growth spurts and development peaks, but not all. In my experience and observation, some of the problem is that when you are striving to be the best in your group and you succeed, you settle down, kick back and enjoy it. Then you watch as others float past you and you are unable to catch up again.

"Only the weak attempts to accomplish what he knows he can already achieve" – Stella Juarez (present) Author

The whole point of training is to get better, to learn new things and to push yourself. There are times when it is appropriate to be the best, but these are when a competition matters, when it is important to be noticed. What will get you there is failure, being second best.

Being second best does not mean that you should settle for second best, nor that you should not strive to be the best, but if you are at the top, you will no longer be pushed as hard. Once you are on this path to success, you need to take yourself out of your comfort zone. It has been stated earlier in this book that practice alone is not enough, which is why I'm not a world class driver.

It needs to be a particular type of practice.

Using the Growth Mindset

"Failure is the foundation of success, and the means by which it is achieved." - Laozi (Zhou Dynasty – 6th century BC) Founder of the Taoist philosophy

To achieve the type of practice that creates the level of development needed to get to the top requires a particular approach. In his book Bounce, Matthew Syed describes how Shizuka Arakawa of Japan, one of the greatest skaters of all time, tumbled over more than 20,000 times in her progression to becoming 2006 Olympic Champion. According to research by Stanford University psychologist Carol Dweck it is because of this growth mindset that she did not interpret falling down as a failure. She interpreted falling down not only as a means of improving, but as evidence that she was improving.

Whether you are a figure skater or a skate boarder, the jumps have to be progressively more difficult and involve some falling down no matter how good you are. You have to be always striving for a better jump.

"Don't wish it were easier. Wish you were better." - Jim Rohn (1930-2009) US entrepreneur, author and motivational speaker

What this means in practice is that you need to find a training group that is better than you, so that not only can you learn from them, but you can strive to become the top of that group. It does not necessarily mean that you have to leave your current group, just that you have to find the ways or the places where you are not the best.

If you are a soccer or rugby player and you are the best of your current team, see if you can train up an age group as well as with your own age group. You need to train with your team but you also need to improve. If training with your team is not getting that improvement, then find another team to train with alongside your current training.

If your training is multi-faceted then find the individuals who are better at each one of the elements and train with them with the aim of getting better than each of them. If you are a runner, find someone who is better at speed-work and train with them for that. Find someone better at endurance and train with them for that. Get better than both in each of their skills.

"If you are afraid of failure, you don't deserve to be successful" – Charles Barkley.(1963-) US NBA Basketball player and TV Analyst

Fundamentally, you might have to put yourself first and change teams or clubs. If you need to go to a team that is a higher level on the whole to achieve your objectives, then that is what you need to do. It is not a question of loyalty. While that is a strong feeling, if you are moving to a stronger club that can improve you more, then it is a rational decision which a decent coach will support (albeit he will obviously be disappointed to lose his star performer). You spend a lot of time in training and your training group will have a huge influence on your development. You need to be sure of two things; that they are the right group for you at any given time and that you are developing at the appropriate pace.

"Opportunity follows struggle. It follows effort. It follows hard work. It doesn't come before." – Shelby Steele (1946-) US Author and documentary film maker

However, it is not just about training. There is also competition. You need to decide what you are prepared to trade off. Would you trade twenty medals and awards at local club level for a single Olympic medal? Of course you would.

So, here is an example, if you are a high-level performer at national level, then your County level competition maybe a little easy. You have a choice. Do you mop up the medals and feel good now, or do you compete up an age group or two to make sure you have serious competition to the extent where you are likely to be beaten? Medals versus progress. Accolades versus development. There should only be one choice if you have a growth mindset.

"Success is a lousy teacher. It seduces smart people into thinking they can't lose" – Bill Gates (1955-) Businessman, founder of Microsoft and formerly the wealthiest man in the world.

Failing Forward

You need to set yourself up to fail. Failure means getting soundly beaten, not only just missing out on a medal. If you have gone up one age group and just been pipped on the line, or just lost by one shot, that will teach you something. But if you are soundly thrashed, you will learn many things. Firstly you have to be mentally strong. It is not easy to put yourself in a position where you are being thrashed, especially if you are a teenager. You can temper this in that there will always be days where you stand out somewhere over the course of the year. Secondly, you will find deficiencies in many areas. You will be beaten on many levels and you will work to improve all of them. Measuring yourself against a mediocre performer tells you little. Instead measure yourself against an elite performer or if not, someone that is significantly better than you. Look at where they are better and start working on narrowing the gap. This is 'failing forward'. Your failures *are* your progress.

Your victories are now not measured in medals, they are measured in progress. If you were 50 points behind, then get to 49, then 48 then 47 and so on. Chip away at the difference. Reward yourself. You do not need medals for mediocrity. You need the bruises of failure.

They are your medals. This is what the growth mindset is. It is how you mentally measure progress rather than measuring outcomes.

"Strength does not come from winning. Your struggles develop your strengths." – Arnold Schwarzenegger (1947-) Actor, bodybuilder and former Mr Universe, Governor of California

Close the Gap

Do not get used to failure though, never accept it as inevitable. Once you put yourself in the position of no longer being the best, you then need to start climbing the ladder. Look to improve at all times. Strive to become the best. Learn as much as possible from the people who are better than you. What do they do that you do not? How do they train, when do they practice? If you can, ask them. If you cannot, then mimic them. Compete with them. Put yourself up against the best all the time. Never take the easy option. 100m World Champion Yohan Blake and Olympic 200m silver medallist Warren Weir would not be as good as they are if they did not train with each other and with Usain Bolt. Usain Bolt would not have won a double triple of Olympic Sprint golds if he did not have Yohan Blake snapping at his heels, not only in competition but in training as well. Each knows that if they do not give 100% every single rep of every single session, then the other will. It's a triple-whammy. You know the other person has worked harder than you have, they have got more out of the training session than you have and they know they have worked harder than you have. Boom! A triple-fold improvement on you. With Blake, Weir and Bolt, they will always push each other on because they know that if they aren't giving their all in training, the person standing next to them in competition will know, because they were there!

Then, when you have learned everything you can from your new training group and your next level up of competition, it is time to move on again. If you fought your way to the top, then find somewhere better where you are at the bottom again. Somewhere where your current level of performance is lower than the people you are training with.

Luke Rowe was a superstar cyclist, winning lots of medals and competitions at a high level as a youth and in his late teens. He became a domestique at Team Sky Pro Cycling. A domestique's role is to protect his star rider from the wind, pace him back to the front if he drops back for any reason, carry his water bottles, food, kit and instructions by dropping back to the team car and then slogging his way back to the star and even giving up his bike if the star has a mechanical fault. For many this would seem like a huge step backwards, one day winning lots of awards and medals, then to sign for a pro team to be a labourer. But being a domestique with the team that won the Tour de France twice is being a fish in a very big pond. This is not starting at the bottom. It is starting at the bottom of the top team in the sport. Being the bottom of the top team is better than being the top of a small team long term. Rowe is learning more from riding with the elite of Team Sky under Sir Dave Brailsford than being the superstar of a team that is competing at national level. He has already taken his first major victory with a stage win in the Tour of Britain.

Your Ego is Your Enemy!

Your ego wants the plaudits of being top dog. But your ego will prevent you from reaching your full potential in sport. Getting the pats on the back, the plaudits and the medals is very pleasant, but you need to learn to wait for those until you have reached the very top, until you are an elite athlete in your sport. You must keep striving all the time to get better, never resting, never being satisfied, enjoying the struggle, not the platitudes of others.

"Remember, if you are not playing your heart out, someone else is. And when you meet him, he will win" – Unknown

Setting yourself up to fail is hard. It is difficult to continuously be struggling to get to the top, especially if you are young. It is nice to be at the top. It is nice to win medals and trophies and accolades. It may also seem that if you are not standing out, then you will not be recognised and get the opportunities. These are both serious issues you need to consider.

You will improve more in the long term if you are with a group that is better than you, even if it means playing up an age group or at a different club. On the other hand, if you are 13 years old, spending the next 7 years struggling to catch up with someone else might not seem that appealing. Do not kid yourself, if you need some markers in there to give you a boost, to give you that recognition that it is all working, then it is okay to take a time out of your development to give your motivation a kick. Compete at your own age group for a short time. Blitz the field. Not only will it give you the recognition of your peers, which can be important especially for teenage boys, it will also give you the boost and confidence that you are doing the right thing. That this struggle is working. It is not a weakness to need that confirmation. There is a difference between needing it for your ego and needing a sanity check on progress. The former is a negative thing, the latter is a positive.

"I have a big-picture outlook, I am willing to fall, and I understand it's ok to fall, but I am going to get back up, I may take a step back, but in the end, I am going to take a giant leap forward." – Tiger Woods (1975-) World No.1 US Professional Golfer and most successful golfer of all time, ranked highest paid athlete in the world.

Getting Recognised

When it comes to recognition and opportunity from higher up in the sport the reality is different. The higher up the ladder you are, the more chance of being recognised for the talent you have. It is a little easier in sports such as track and field, where your numbers are absolutes, but in a team sport, scouts are more interested in whether a player can perform at their level. They will not see that if a player is scoring 10 goals against a mediocre opposition. It might allow you to move into the next level up, the District or the County level, but it will not be until you perform at that level that anyone will truly be able to assess your ability. It is how you cope with playing against the best opposition that counts. Scouts are generally very good at what they do. They do not look for the same things parents do. You might not score and nothing seemed to go right, but a scout would look at how you coped, how you created space, what you did for the team, what you contributed and what you saw in the game; in other words your potential. They are operating at a different level and looking for different things. It can also work the other way of course, you may think you had a fantastic game and scored three goals and the scout might look and think the team would have scored six if you had made better decisions.

Summary

If you want to succeed you have to be operating at the level that the scouts and talent spotters are working at. Learning to compete at the highest level means you will start off by failing at that level. To show you can play or compete at the highest level, you have to be at there. You cannot play safe, you have to attempt to play at the next level and compete at that level. Don’t try to fit in if you step up a level, **stand out!** Don't show respect to anyone that you're competing against, get in there and try to beat them even if you don't think you can. That is what will keep you in there, earn you respect and get you noticed.

1. Find a team, club or training group that is better than you are

2. Strive to learn everything you can from that training group

3. Become the best of that training group

4. Find another training group that is better than you are

5. Compete, do not just win.

6. Take an occasional checkpoint of progress by competing at your own level.

CHAPTER 17

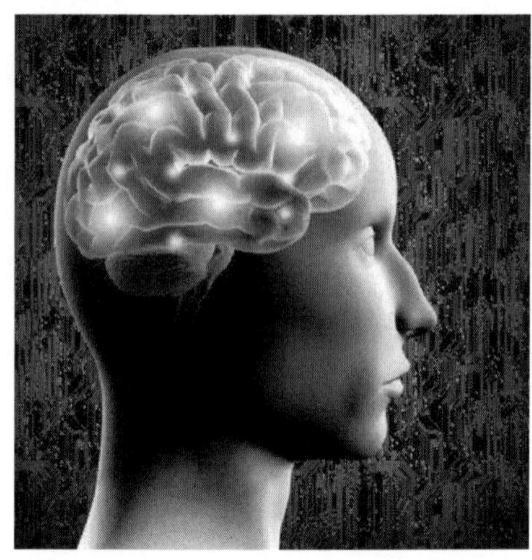

MIND GAMES

Once you get to the highest level, the margins of difference between performers are generally very small. There may be an outstanding performer in a particular generation who changes the boundaries, such as Usain Bolt, Lionel Messi, Dick Fosbury, or Tiger Woods, but other than these the differences between performers are marginal.

After all, their training is similar, their knowledge is similar, the amount of training they've completed in terms of the thousands of hours of practice is similar and the laws of physics are the same for everyone. If you took most professional golfers onto a course, in the same conditions individually, with no fans and no competitors then they would all score pretty much the same. However, the difference is that as soon as there is a trophy at stake, with millions of people watching, prize money and competition the result change. What makes the difference? Simply, it is how each competitor not only handles the event itself in their own mind, but their impact on how the other competitors handle the event.

Thinking inside and outside the box

The mental side of sport becomes the factor that makes the difference in performance. Take another example. A footballer paid £100,000 plus per week should be able to score a penalty 99 times out of a 100, with the one failure being when the goalkeeper guessed everything right. In training this is probably not far off (factoring in the goalkeeper's increased knowledge of the player). However, in cup finals, the percentage of goals scored from penalties becomes greatly reduced. Once the fans, the consequences, and the pressure of the competitive situation come into play the player starts to over-think. This is often because the player has returned to conscious competence where they can no longer perform unconsciously; they are effectively choking. They have too long to think, the expectation is that they will score, the odds are in their favour. Usually, an elite player is continuously updating competitive situations and game pictures. They are used to responding and reacting at incredible speeds and making lightning fast decisions, then suddenly, the whole world stops while they compose themselves. It is not even a skill that can be practised in training particularly as the defining success factor is the handling of the pressure of the situation something that cannot be replicated in training. Most fans cannot understand how a player can miss a penalty. Unless you have been in the situation then you will not. Penalties are missed regularly and the higher profile the game, the greater the probability of a miss.

Influencing Others

On top of all this internal pressure, there is the external pressure from your competitors. A skilled competitor will try to influence your mental state, some subtly, some not so subtly. A fantastic and none too subtle version of affecting your opposition's mental state would be to continue the football penalty theme. In the 1984 European Cup Final between Liverpool and AS Roma the game was level after extra time. Outside of a World Cup match the pressure-cooker of penalties in the European Cup Final is probably as extreme as it gets in professional football. First, as Bruno Conti prepared to take his kick, the Liverpool goalkeeper, Bruce Grobelaar, started pretending to eat the goal net as if it was spaghetti. Conti duly missed, firing his kick over the bar. At the next penalty, Francesco Graziani had to watch as Grobelaar acted as if he had wobbly legs, feigning comic terror as Graziani was about to take his kick. Graziani also missed. Liverpool went on to win the penalty shoot-out 4-2.

"Serious sport has nothing to do with fair play. It is bound up with hatred, jealousy, boastfulness, disregard of all rules and sadistic pleasure in witnessing violence. In other words, it is what without the shooting." - George Orwell, Author (1903-1950)

I had the opportunity to talk to Olympic 100m Gold-medallist Linford Christie OBE recently about his achievements, and he related that his rival, nine-time Olympic Gold medallist Carl Lewis, used to go up to all his competitors in the call up room just before the start and shake their hand. According to Christie this was Lewis' way of imposing himself on them, as if the race had already finished and Lewis had already won, thanks for coming. He was mentally affecting the other runners' preparation and putting it in their minds that they were only here as part of the Carl Lewis show.

In the 1993 World Championships, Christie was having none of it and instead stared Lewis down, somewhat like a boxer pre-fight. Christie said there was then a stand-off where Lewis stood with his hand out and Christie simply stared at Lewis and refused to take it. The uncomfortable stand-off was only broken when Christie barked at Lewis like a dog, making the startled Lewis jump backwards and then wander off. Christie subsequently won the 100m final.

In his first autobiography, 'In Pursuit of Glory', many time Olympic Gold-medallist , Sir Bradley Wiggins describes a similar thing in the Athens Olympics in 2004.

He broke the World Record in the first qualifying round. "You can't ride a 4:15 without it hurting badly; you are on the edge of what the body can do and cope with. But as I rolled around afterwards, I wasn't going to let anyone know exactly how much that hurt. On the contrary, I was going to showboat a bit and let them think that was just a stroll in the park. I cruised around smiling, without a care in the world, fighting the desire to collapse in a heap and vomit"

Players will also try to put each other off with put downs and 'trash-talk' during games, known in the UK as 'sledging'. Mohammed Ali was a master of this. Many players attempt it. The best ones can really get under other people's skin. Sometimes nothing is out of bounds (although Chelsea FC's John Terry found there are limits when his 'banter' became racist abuse). It can backfire, though, as when cricketer Glen Mcgrath asked Eddo Brandes why he was so fat, to receive the answer "Because every time I sleep with your wife she gives me a biscuit".

Another way of affecting your competition is to be more subtle. If the competitor does not like the pressure then increasing that can affect their performance. This involves giving their inner chimp (see Chapter 19) a good shake to get them going. Add to all the things the chimp would worry about in order to give it some support in waking up and taking hold. On the other hand it might be to tell them how well you have trained, how confident you are, or how good your competitors are looking. The whole point of this is to disrupt their preparation process and make them think about something else, to make them think about their performance, to wake their chimp, become emotional, and react differently to the way they have trained themselves to react. This is not to say that you have to do this, but it is a perfectly reasonable part of competition.

How far you go is dependent on your sport and your own ethics, but it is very important to know what happens and how to spot when someone is attempting to influence you for their competitive advantage. If this is the case, you can recognise it, shut down your chimp and get back to your preparation. If you are skilled enough you can even turn it back around on your competitor.

Sometimes the influence is more physical. Individuals or teams try to dominate others physically, usually outside the rules. Pushes and shoves out of sight of the referee, nudges during your approach, walking across your path, getting in the way. Sometimes, if the sport allows it, the approach might even be more bruising. Some teams play very physically and opposing teams know they will come away bruised and battered. This can affect their game-plan and cause them to play into the other team's hands, and it is not always the obvious sports like football or rugby where this is found most. Mo Farah CBE, the World and Olympic 5000m and 10000m champion, is often subject to physical abuse in high profile races to try to affect his performance: elbows, pushes, and spikes in the calves and shins are not uncommon. Usain Bolt relates this about his competitor Justin Gatlin. "I ran once with him in Zagreb. We were walking back and forward and he actually spat across my lane. I know he was trying to intimidate me".

Putting on a Show

Whether or not you actively participate in mind games, showing your competitors a carefully constructed ambience is very important. This gives your competitors the impression that you want them to have. Would you like them to see you as a nervous gibbering wreck before a competition? Clearly not, so if you have prepared effectively with your anchors and you have got yourself into the 'zone' as I described in Chapter 12, then you won't be a gibbering wreck anyway, but how you feel and what you want your competitors to see don't have to be the same thing.

There are many different ambiences you could give off to influence your competition but you need to select one that is closest to your personality. The more genuine it is, the better you will be able to act it. In your early development you can try some roles on for size and see how they fit for you. Here are some famous examples:

Sir Nick Faldo MBE is famous for being a cool, unemotional, machine of a golfer, never making mistakes; everything looks like it is part of the plan. That is how he wanted his competition to see him. It was very intimidating for them even though there was nothing aggressive in what he did. Faldo did not engage with the other golfers and never chatted to them. In the 1996 final round of the Masters championship Greg Norman's performance spectacularly collapsed, with Faldo reeling him in on the leaderboard, making no mistakes, increasing the pressure on Norman with each hole. A persona and a style of play built up over years led Norman to feel a pressure that was created by Faldo.

Usain Bolt is the exact opposite, very relaxed, chatty, and seemingly unfocused. In the Olympic games in London in the 100m final, there was huge pressure on Bolt after being beaten by Yohan Blake in the Jamaican trials and false starting in the World Championships. How did Bolt react to this pressure? By laughing and joking with the gamesmakers, mugging for the TV camera, and generally fooling around. But as sprint legend turned TV pundit Michael Johnson has said previously, when the starter calls, there will be no-one more focussed than Bolt. This is his routine and it unsettles some of his competitors. Should they be more relaxed, is he taking it seriously? Suddenly, they are thinking about Bolt and not their own race.

Boxer Mike Tyson was different again. In such a sport as boxing, being able to intimidate opponents to the point of fear should be very difficult, especially if you are a young, relatively short fighter who is new to the scene. Yet, Tyson scared other fighters. His fighting style was extremely explosive and he was one of the hardest punchers around. He avoided all the finery and glitz and glamour that most fighters employed. He wore plain black shorts and plain black shoes that were shorter than normal. When he came to the ring, he did not have a retinue of people around him, just his cornermen. He did not have flashy music. Mike Tyson is here on business was his message. He came to fight and he fought hard (and he fought often – more than most of his contemporaries). Most of his fights were knock-outs. If you watch his fights you can see the fear of some of his opponents. Big men, heavyweight boxers were scared of this young man. His ambience had a huge impact. He won the fight before he had even left the changing rooms.

"I want to rip out his heart and feed it to Lennox Lewis. I want to kill people. I want to rip their stomachs out and eat their children." - Mike Tyson, Boxer, former undisputed heavyweight champion of the world. (1966 - present)

Mohammed Ali was another boxer who employed yet a different mental tactic. He told his opponents that he was the greatest; he went for all the flash and glitz. He made a show of everything from the interviews with his poetry that put down his opponents, to the fight itself. He fought differently to everyone else, using his upper body and head speed to avoid punches instead of the traditional method of blocking them. Ali even went as far as regularly predicting the round he would win the fight in, usually in rhyme.

"I done wrestled with an alligator, I done tussled with a whale; handcuffed lightning, thrown thunder in jail; only last week, I murdered a rock, injured a stone,

hospitalised a brick; I'm so mean I make medicine sick." - Mohammed Ali (1942-) Former professional boxer and considered by many as the greatest heavyweight of all time

It is not just individuals who can use mental pressure to defeat opponents. Sir Alex Ferguson's Manchester United not only dominated English football for over a decade between 1991 and 2013 winning 13 Premier League titles and countless other trophies, but they have also consistently mentally dominated opponents and officials. The team never settled for a draw, never knew when they are beaten. Teams playing against them actually played more nervously when they were in front. When Manchester United were behind, they would increase the pressure with a continuous onslaught of attacks. This pressure increased towards the last few minutes of the game as the clock ticked down. Each game was played like a cup final. Most teams played the long road and even if they are challenging for the title accept that some draws and losses are inevitable. Manchester United did not play this way. Every goal against them was an affront. Every decision against them was an affront. They expected to win. They always played like they would win in the end.

Teams playing against them in the 1990's played as if they would lose even if they were winning with only a few minutes to go. Sir Alex Ferguson's watch was famous – if United were behind, he starts the pressure on the referee to clock every stoppage to ensure the maximum amount of time available for them to complete the victory. United have maintained a fantastic level of players, but the sum of the parts was always greater than the whole and the number of last minute victories over the years that United have won is legendary, well beyond a statistical norm. The most famous is the 1999 Champions League Final against Bayern Munich. With 90 minutes up, United 1-0 behind and the game essentially over, Manchester United won 2-1 with two goals in injury time. It is further testament to the nature of this side that any other team in football would have accepted the first goal to set up extra-time and then regrouped for the additional 30 minutes of play. But Manchester United refused to get beaten.

Polishing Your Act

As you can see from the examples above, mental competition is an important part of any sport and, at the highest levels, can be the only difference between two opponents. Players influence and intimidate opponents with the ambiance they create. It can be an approach that varies game by game, or it can be a continuous influence that creates an expectation level that is almost too powerful to resist.

Once you get to the top level, you will be part of this mental game, whether you like it or not. Whether you are a player or a pawn, you are on the board. Therefore, it is important to get this side of your performance perfected early. Dr Steve Peters, the psychologist who works with British Cycling and Liverpool FC, describes your ‘ambience’ as a mixture of your demeanour, stance, and the way in which you interact with others, but the ambience is something that can be chosen.

First, you need to decide what kind of player you are. This needs to be close to your natural character, so if you are feisty and talkative then use that to your advantage. If you are quiet and controlled then use that. There's no right and wrong in this aspect of the game, so you might as well do something you are comfortable with and work with your natural character.

If you do not want to engage in the games yourself, you need to build up your defence to everyone else's games. Practice performing under distracting circumstances. Get people in training to try to put you off. Linford Christie OBE strongly believes in the mental aspects of sport and now part of his training with the athletes he coaches is to ensure that the banter level is very high. The athletes abuse each other and try to put each other off continuously, so that at events there is nothing that can be said to them that has not been said to them many times before in training. In fact it makes the race more like training. They are strong and immune.

Second, if you want to be more active at mental games then like any other part of your sport you need to practice. You need to develop your skill, find out what works and what doesn't. Remember that this is an extreme version of you and it is only an act, which is part of the game. You need to maintain the act when necessary, but it doesn't mean you have to become that person in your life. As part of your practice, modelling the behaviour of someone that has the aura you want to portray is a good way to practice.

Mindset Modelling

A great way to develop that is through mindset modelling, which was developed by John Grinder and Richard Bandler, the creators of Neuro Linguistic Programming, in the mid 1970's. The purpose of modelling is to basically model yourself on someone else who behaves in the way that you want to behave. One athlete's weakness is another athlete's strength. Mindset modelling takes advantage of this. It works on the principle that if one person can do it, anyone can do it. So by working out how someone else does something and then learning how to do it yourself, you are essentially modelling that individual's behaviour.

So find someone, a teammate or elite athlete who seems to create the aura that you would like to have. Let us say that you want to show others a supremely confident aura ahead of competition. This goes beyond feeling confident yourself, which I covered in Chapter 12. It is acting a part for others to see. Whom do you know who is like that whom you have access to? Why are they so self-assured? How do they approach the event? What are they thinking about?

Follow the steps below to learn how to project your aura to others.

1. Identify the behaviour you want to model. What do you need to change to become a better athlete?

2. Find someone who behaves the way you want to. It can be someone famous or a teammate; the level of performance does not matter, only the behaviour.

3. Analyse what he or she does in situations that you want to model. What do they say and how do they interact with others and their environment? Ask **yourself** what they think about and how they feel. If you have access to them then ask them.

4. Once you have the answers you are looking for, play the role your model plays and notice how it works for you. Act like them, feel like them, and talk like them. Do this until you are no longer modelling a person and your new behaviour has become a habit.

Remember that in modelling, you are only seeing a behaviour, and that behaviour is just an image you want to portray to others. The person you may be modelling may be exactly like you with the same internal turmoil, but they exude calm. It does not matter what goes on inside, the mental game is all about what other people see.

Summary

How you are influenced by your competitors and how you influence them can be a key element in your performance. Learn the techniques and practice them to add another competitive weapon to your armoury.

1. Be aware of mental techniques and especially the ones that your competitors can and will use against you.

2. Actively manage your ‘ambience’

3. Model the behaviour of how you want to be perceived.

4. Practice, practice, practice.

Part 3 – Dealing with obstacles

CHAPTER 18

WAYPOINTS AND DESTINATIONS

"You have got to be careful if you don't know where you're going, because you might not get there" – Yogi Berra (1925-) US Baseball player and manager

If you were ever a boy scout, have done orienteering, or simply know how to use maps for routes, then you will probably be familiar with the use of waypoints. When you plan a route, you have a start point (today) and you have a destination (in this case, your dream). Getting from one to the other will have natural waypoints, which are large and small milestones along the way that you believe you have to pass through to get to the destination. This is all perfectly natural and absolutely correct. To get from one point to another, you will have to pass through other points. To get from one level of performance to another you will need to pass through other levels. So far so good.

Waypoints are NOT Destinations

The first principle is that **waypoints are disposable**. Every waypoint must be subordinate to the destination. Waypoints help in planning but they are not critical to the achievement of the destination. This is very important. It is useful to plan the waypoints to give you a route, but you can discard them if they no longer fit, or if the route needs to change. Your dream is where you are heading; your route there is nothing more than a prediction, a forecast. You cannot predict the future, you must adapt to things that change, and change is inevitable.

Failure to achieve a marker (as a waypoint) at a point in the future gives no indication as to the potential for the overall achievement of your dream. If you have read about others in your sport or outside who have been successful, you will see that rarely do people take a direct route to the top. If you were to map out an ideal route and see how many people followed it, you would find the total to be close to zero. Truly successful people are very adaptable.

The second principle is that waypoints should only be seen as relative to the destination, not as an end in themselves. Too much focus on the waypoint can negatively affect the destination, and you need to avoid doing this.

Having a target for the season is perfectly normal and correct. But that target must be sacrificed if it's no longer necessary to achieve the end destination. If there is a trade-off to be made, the long term gains should always win.

"To be able at any moment, to sacrifice what we are, for what we would become" – Maharishi Mahesh Yogi (1918-2008) Meditation Guru and Spiritual Leader

Let's start with a simple example of a car journey. If you were travelling from Glasgow to London, you might decide that the best way to get from one point to the other is to pass through Leeds and Nottingham and to maybe have an hour's rest in Leeds. So your destination is London and the waypoints are Leeds and Nottingham, with Leeds being the big one.

Now let us say that there are roadworks in Nottingham and your fancy SatNav tells you that there is a better route. Do you take the diversion? Of course you would.

What if there is a major accident on the A1 that means you are stuck and do not get to Leeds when you thought you would. Does the delay mean you have failed to reach your destination? Only if you decide not to go there any more, if you turn around and go back.

"You have to have a contingency plan for adversity because you're going to face it. Period. Your only choice is how you respond to it." - Jon Gruden, former NFL Coach of the Oakland Raiders and Tampa Bay Buccaneers (1963-present)

Again, there is a major delay and you decide stopping in Leeds is no longer necessary; you decide to do a couple of short stops along the way instead of one big one. How does this affect your destination?

Finally, the delays on the way to London are so great that the **reason** you were heading there would not be relevant any more. You are going shopping for the weekend and you would lose too much time so you divert to Manchester. In this case, the overriding reason for the destination takes priority not only over the waypoint but over the purpose.

Why is this relevant? Who wants to go to London shopping? I'm a sportsman/woman! The examples were important to understand the difference between a waypoint and a destination. The destination and the purpose of the destination are the things that should be the most important in your approach and philosophy. So let us put this into a sporting context.

"If opportunity doesn't knock, build a door." - Milton Berle (1908-2002) US Comedian and Actor

Taking a Long View

Plans are predictions, they are routes to get somewhere, but you must be flexible enough to change them, as you cannot predict the future. Track and Field has some quite specific timings so these will make a good example. In the first instance, to put diverting around Nottingham in a sporting context, in track and field qualifying for the major championships requires the qualifying times or distances to be done in a specific window. Most athletes and coaches will build to a specific event(s) to get the qualification. It is an important waypoint. But as long as it is an official meet (and pretty much all events are official) then which meet is irrelevant to the qualification. If you planned on an event in May and felt good at an event in April then go for it. You never know what will happen in May. Get the time in the bag, miss the road block. If it doesn't happen, you can still go for it in May. Does this change the overall destination or direction? Not at all. You may think that this seems too obvious, but some people plan so specifically and so rigidly that they would not go for April.

"Don't make the small things into big things and don't let the big things become small things. Never get too carried away with the highs and never get overwhelmed by the lows". - Shane Sutton, the coach of Tour de France and 6-time Olympic medallist Sir Bradley Wiggins

Your major road block on the A1 causing a delay could be an injury. If you miss your target this year, then change it. Change the timescale. If you do it next year, does that mean you' will never get to your destination? Of course not. This year is your plan, but it does not have to be this year. It does not have to be this event or that event. If you follow this line, what may be a minor injury could easily become a major one because you are so focussed on a particular moment that you play on. If you think that would not happen, or that your coach would protect you from that, then you may be mistaken. The injury to Robert Griffin III in the 2013 American Football play-off game between the Washington Redskins and Seattle Seahawks in January is a recent and high profile case in point, where both athlete and coach failed to prevent this from happening. Griffin's knee buckled in the first 15 minutes of the game. He played on because he believed that is what you should do. His coach let him play on despite his clear injury. It was expected, because the game was "important".

The result was that the Redskins lost and more importantly, the 22 year old (note that it wasn't even that he would never have another opportunity, this was his first professional season), had anterior cruciate ligament (ACL) reconstruction and a repair to a torn lateral collateral ligament. At the time of writing, the hope was that this surgery was successful but it would be 8 months before he made a full recovery. Would it have been better if he hadn't continued playing? Who can say, but the moral of this story is that both the athlete and coach can get carried away with a short term gain and chasing immediate glory and lose sight of the long term impact. You may think that at the lower levels of sport this is less likely, but you would be wrong. I have seen many examples of people performing through injury and making themselves worse.

If you pick up an injury, take the longer view; protect the destination, not the waypoint. There is always time. The chapter on dealing with injury will help you cope, but you have to be in the right mindset to make the call in the first place.

For our third example we took a few shorter stops along the way instead of a longer waypoint in Leeds. Using track and field as an example again, often, up to the age of 18, most track and field athletes will target the English Schools Championships. There will be an equivalent peak championship in every sport. Missing the English Schools, for whatever reason, or under-performing could be caused by anything: an injury in the build up, getting your peak wrong, or something as innocuous as getting a cold the day before the first round. Even, dare we consider it, you might choke in the event.

As bitterly disappointing as this would be, this is not the time to flush away your season or your destination. In track and field, the English Schools in July is a big event, but, if you miss this for some reason, then there are still the Outdoor National (AAA) Championships in August. In addition, the athlete rankings (Power of 10) shows who is the top performer in all events, not just one, and are collected across the whole year. If you won the AAA's and topped the rankings for the year, would this be enough? There are some variables you cannot control. But you cannot let them control you either and it pays to keep them in perspective. There are no absolutes.

Finally, and more arbitrary, is the change of the destination as a reaction to circumstances. If you are following the steps in this book and have a clear understanding of your motivation there may be a time when your destination changes because you have a new dream. Shelley Rudman was a very good sprint hurdler who dreamed of the Olympics. She is now an Olympic medallist and World Champion, except not in sprinting. She is at the top of her sport in Skeleton Bobsleigh. Shelley is from Pewsey in deepest Wiltshire and it would be fair to say that this is not a global powerhouse in the skeleton bobsleigh world. But Rudman is living her dream, even though it is not the same as she originally started with.

Would you take that? Being the top of a sport that you hadn't originally set out to do? Manchester instead of London?

The destination is all about your dream and your motivation to achieve your dream. If you cannot see the forest for the trees, then the destination can get lost. You might lose your way. There is also the danger that you can lose focus and motivation. As explained in Chapter 5, people can also get caught up in thinking they have made it once the accolades start, once they have made the team, or achieved national prominence. They start to see the waypoint as an end in itself. Suddenly, they start making money, are in demand from sponsors, and are on TV. They are getting attention.

In his book The Talent Code, Daniel Coyle writes about effort-based learning and outcome based learning. This is based on the work by Carol Dweck that was described earlier in this book. Dweck proposes that people exercise either a fixed mindset or a growth mindset.

In a fixed mindset, people believe their basic qualities, like their intelligence or talent, are simply fixed traits. They spend their time documenting their intelligence or talent instead of developing them. They also believe that talent alone creates success – without effort. They're wrong.

In a growth mindset, people believe that their most basic abilities can be developed through dedication and hard work – brains and talent are just the starting point. This view creates a love of learning and resilience that is essential for great accomplishment. Virtually all great people have these qualities.

If you have a fixed mindset then once you have 'arrived' you are cashing in on your talent. People have recognised your abilities and you can ease off. You have achieved what your talent deserves. You stop learning and stop improving.

"You'll never know when you'll have a breakthrough... Could be today, tomorrow or a year from now but you'll never know if you break" – Lolo Jones (1982-) US 100 and 60 metre Hurdler and World Indoor Champion and Bobsled World Champion

Summary

There are no absolutes in the journey to your dream. You cannot predict the future. You can plan a route and Chapter 11 explains how to prepare, but you have to be prepared to step over and around obstacles. Find a different door if one closes, and occasionally climb through a window.

1. Identify a 'rough-cut' route to get to your dream, with the things you have identified you want to achieve along the way

2. Write down the approximate timing along the way.

3. Add a 'tolerance' to the timings – be pragmatic and make it as wide as possible – plus or minus a year for example.

4. Now add a fallback – if not that event, then are there others I can target within my tolerance band.

5. Finally, be realistic – how important are the targets to the end goal? Are they 'nice to have' because they are good indicators for you personally, or is it

genuinely impossible to get to the next stage without completing this one?

Chapter 19

Managing Poor Performance

So, you have your dream, you are motivated, and you know why you want to be successful. As renowned motivational speaker and author Eric Thomas would say, "You want success as bad as you want to breathe". It's all going well, everyone tells you how good you are.

And then the wheels fall off.

How to cope when the wheels fall off

More often than not, it will seem that they will fall off at the worst possible time or when you and everyone else wants success the most, when it is most important that you perform. Poor performance happens. It happens for many reasons and the most important thing with poor performance is to be able to learn from it and then forget it. In this chapter I will explain to you how to control the factors affecting performance, how to prevent the ones that can be prevented, and how to handle poor performance when it happens.

"Often when things are at their worst, you're closer than you can imagine to success." - Bill Walsh, former US Football Coach of the San francisco 49ers (1931 - 2007)

There are two types of poor performance, a long term loss of form or a short term dip. A long term loss of form is usually caused by a specific incident, such as injury or an external event such as loss of a family member that may impact motivation and desire, or it could be a regular developmental dip. When young people are on a high development trajectory in sport it is often in parallel with their physical development.

Performance Plateau

The adolescent performance plateau is one most kids experience. Often it doesn't necessarily result in a loss of form, but will look like one because everyone else is improving. It is important to be aware of how most people develop through their teens. Depending on the sport, there may be lots of ups and downs during growth spurts when coordination can deteriorate for a short time. During these periods, some kids are suddenly bigger than others and their performance relative to each other can change drastically. During this time, you just have to keep ploughing on. I have covered this extensively in Chapter 9. At this point the direction needs to be important. You can experience huge discrepancies between players that spring up suddenly. Eventually the development will level out and what will remain will be the hard-earned talent.

"Many of life's failures are people who did not realise how close they were to success when they gave up." - Thomas Edison (1847-1931) US Inventor, most famous for inventing the electric light bulb

In Chapter 9 I explained the differences between athletes who had the advantages of being born at the beginning of the age cycle and those at the end, and how they must adapt differently. But for both groups, once the growth has slowed right down and the rate of physical development diminishes, everyone ends up around the same place (allowing for genetics differences and all else being equal). This is when the 10,000 hour rule comes to the fore and when all that practice comes into its own.

There are three lessons from early development. First, everyone will plateau to some extent once physical development slows right down in the late teens. You have had an extra factor in your development that suddenly drops out. You may even go backwards for a year or so. This is normal.

Second, no matter where you are today in your development relative to your peers, you need to take a long view, look to the under 17 or under 20 age groups for when you start to come through instead of now.

Third, take the advantages you are given and work hard to stay out in front.

"Never measure the height of a mountain, until you have reached the top. Then you will see how low it was." - Dag Hammarskjöld (1905-1961) Swedish diplomat, economist, and author

Whether you are an early or late developer, you will work through a plateau or at the very least a slowing down of the development trajectory where your physical development has slowed to a crawl and you have diminishing returns. You cannot keep taking a second off your 100m time! Preparing for this and understanding it will help you get through it. If you have been at the top of the tree developmentally during your formative years, then this will come as a shock. The late developers have a distinct advantage in that they are conditioned to working their way through and taking a long view. Sometimes this can have an extreme effect on the early developers and they all too often flare out and give in rather than adapt.

The key to controlling a performance plateau is in understanding. It happens to everyone at some point. How it affects you is completely related to your frame of mind. You have not peaked, you have hit a point where your gains become much more difficult and so the rate of improvement has slowed considerably. Be patient and work through it. It will often take a year or a season to break through it but you have to have confidence that you will. This is tough to handle at an age when there are other stressful situations such as exams and education choices. Accept it as inevitable and work through it. Gains are small during this period, so work harder at your sport if necessary. Step up what you do and introduce all the things that you aren't currently doing that you learned from your earlier research. Be aware though, this will limit the time in the plateau but not eliminate it.

Performance Dips and How to Prevent Them

Now that you understand an inevitable stage in your age development I can move onto the seemingly random and unexpected dips in performance, where there is a short term loss of form or the days when things just do not go right. This can either be because of factors seemingly out of your control, such as conditions, opposition, or a random event that affected your performance. It could be that you just choked.

"The only person who can beat me is me." – Michael Johnson (1967-) Four-time Olympic gold medallist and current 400m world record holder

Nerves cause some poor performance. A level of anxiety is normal, as anxiety and excitement have essentially the same physiological effect, they are both 'aroused states'. It is the emotional perspective that is different, whether you feel 'bad' or 'good'. Reversal Theory is a field of psychology dealing with the dynamic qualities of an experience. It describes how a person regularly switches between feelings like anxiety or excitement depending on the meaning they attach to a given situation at a given time. Reversal Theory allows the possibility of being able to switch between these psychological states. Traditionally, the accepted response to someone who is anxious is to tell them to calm down, but this state is a long way from anxiety, which is an aroused state, and the switch is difficult to achieve. However, switching from anxiety to excitement is relatively easy as they are the same state, with slightly different meanings attached.

Generally, feeling anxiety or excitement is triggered by one of two states, which then dictates the experience that you attach to them. A *telic* state emphasises end goals, and you are motivated by achieving a particular outcome. Those in a telic state are more likely to experience the arousal as anxiety. A *paratelic* state emphasises the process and is more playful, spontaneous, and focused on the present moment. In a paratelic state you are more likely to experience arousal as enjoyment or excitement. You will see from previous chapters how closely linked this is to the growth and fixed mindset model.

To overcome nerves and feelings of anxiousness follow these steps:

1. Focus on the process. You will understand waypoints and destinations and you will also understand fixed and growth mindsets. Try not to think about what happens later, think about what you are doing now, the process you are going through. Get in the zone which is entirely geared to how you perform not what you achieve.

2. Find the positives. If you have had the same experience before, find the positives in it. You survived, you have got to this one, so it cannot have been all bad. Focus on the positives in the experience you have already had.

3. Create a trigger. Nerves are debilitating, so you need to overcome them. It may seem obvious but you need to recognise the difference between nervous anxiety and excitement. What is the feeling that you experience that means you are definitely anxious. This may be shaking hands, cold sweats or shallow breathing. Once you know what it is, then use that feeling as a trigger to reassess your state of arousal and to go to work on steps 1 and 2.

4. Modify your language. When you talk about the situation that makes you nervous, such as a particular event, then consciously talk about how you'll compete, not about how it will end or what you will achieve. Focus on the process when you speak, not the outcome. Use humour to talk about what you are about to do. Being playful resonates better with the paratelic state.

Preparation

To reduce the likelihood of a dip in performance you need to follow a tried and trusted routine. There is comfort in familiarity. All of my athletes prepare for competition in the same way each time. It is not necessarily the same for each of them, but it is similar. They have a routine that starts at the last training session before competition and then follows through what they eat, when they start the warm up, and the sequence of the warm up. Then everything remains consistent right to the point where they are in the 'set' position on the track. They practice the warm-up on the last training session, every time, no matter how many times they have done it before. Everything is routine, everything then becomes normal. Their thought process should also be the same. We allow for variables, like different call-up durations, but we will always aim to get to a venue in plenty of time, so that the warm-up clock starts ticking at an exact time before the call-up so that we are in the routine. Tour de France cyclist and multi-Olympic Gold Medallist Sir Bradley Wiggins does exactly the same thing. He has a set routine which he goes through, the same every time, mentally and physically, so that when he is at the start he knows he's ready, because he has been ready every single other time he has followed that process.

Dealing with Poor Performance

"Opportunity often comes disguised in the form of misfortune, or temporary defeat." - Napolean Hill (1883-1970) Author

Sometimes, all the preparation still does not result in a perfect performance. You might be disappointed with the result. Rather than dwell on it and let it eat away at you, fuelling your chimp, you need to process it and move on. The sooner you process this, the better. The method I like to use is as follows:

Take a piece of paper and write on it everything that contributed to your performance not being as you expected. Include everything you can think of. It might not just be about what you did; it can and should include what other people did.

Now take the list and assign an A and a B to every item. Items should be assigned an A if it is within your control. Be careful here to make sure you are taking responsibility appropriately. If you set off late and then hit traffic which meant you couldn't follow your normal warm up procedure, then that is your responsibility. You cannot control the traffic but did you set off early enough? If you had allowed extra time however and still not made it in time, then you can only be realistic, otherwise you would arrive the week before! In this case it would be allocated a B. The B's are for the things that you could not have controlled; your competitors, the organisers and so on.

Now write these onto two separate pieces of paper, one for the A's and one for the B's. Do a last check that the B's couldn't be controlled and then screw that list up and throw it away. If you could have no influence on them, then there is no point worrying about them, so throw it away and forget about them.

Now you have a list of the things you could have done better or controlled more, you can deal with each item. Depending on how much improvement you want to make, you can apply the 80/20 rule or rank them in order of the impact on your performance. Once you have decided which ones you need to change, if not all of them, decide what you are going to do differently next time. Then implement your actions and start to prepare for the next time you compete.

Summary

Preparation is the key to preventing poor performance. If you prepare the same each time the result should be the same. If it isn't, look at the reasons it isn't and then deal with the ones that you can. Don't stew on them and don't leave anything to chance. Resolve it for next time so it won't happen again, and then you won't have to worry about it.

1. If you are a younger athlete, your development will slow down at some point. Be prepared for it.

2. Be aware of the advantages your development age has on you and work with it, do not rely on it, or be overwhelmed by it.

3. Write your lists, improve what you can improve and discard the things you have no control over.

CHAPTER 20

CHOKING AND HOW TO PREVENT IT

Another example of poor performance is what is known as choking. This can happen over a very short space of time, such as a single shot, a single event or match, or it can continue for a while. To understand how to prevent it and to overcome it if it happens you need to understand what is happening to you when you choke.

The danger of thinking

To achieve a high level of sport you need to practice until your performance becomes natural. You need to be practised to the level where people think you have a natural talent (although you now know this is due to practice and there is nothing natural about it). As I explained in Chapter 10, the progression to this point starts from unconscious incompetence (I do not know that I cannot do it), to conscious incompetence (I know I cannot do it), through to conscious competence (I can now do it but I have to concentrate) and finally to unconscious competence (I can do it without thought). When you are very good you operate at the unconscious competence zone where your mind and body work in harmony and respond quickly without you having to think about it. You are thinking ahead, not thinking about reacting to what is happening in real time. It is the equivalent of the tennis player thinking about how they are going to manoeuvre their opponent into the position where the point can be won, rather than considering where to move after the opponent has served.

To be in the zone that I described in the chapter on mental preparation, you must be operating at the unconscious competence level. You are playing with a feeling that things are happening for you without thinking. Choking is where there is something that has snapped you out of this level, the pressure of a particular shot or particular game that takes you back to conscious competence. It is the opposite of nerves that I described in Chapter 17. Nerves is more about not thinking or not thinking rationally. Choking is suddenly thinking about something you wouldn't normally think about, how you play the game or how you perform a specific action.

"Concentration is the ability to think about absolutely nothing when it is absolutely necessary." - Ray Knight, former US Baseball player for Cincinnati Reds and New York Mets (1952-present)

Something has triggered you to start thinking. It may be that you were happily delivering your performances and then your coach or a parent says that this is a really important game for whatever reason. Perhaps a scout is watching, you are on camera, or it's the final. So you need to be even better. It might be one missed shot that you cannot let go, and so you are now concentrating on how to make the next one. The next one also misses so you concentrate harder; things get worse.

Choking is confusing and distressing because the shot you have played a hundred times, a thousand times and was very easy to you is suddenly difficult. You are doing all the same things, but it is no longer working. The harder you try the worse it gets.

Your conscious brain is getting involved where it has no right to be involved. You have started considering what you are doing in real time. The very thing that makes you so good, your unconscious competence, has now been switched off and you have taken a step back to conscious competence. This is a level below where you were before. The more you concentrate, the worse it gets because you are adding in more and more conscious thought.

Breaking a Choke

So how do you break a choke? There are some theories and academic studies into this and often they involve prevention. Training under pressure or anxiety will reduce the chances of choking due to pressure or anxiety in a match or event. However, I believe that most of the situations that create the choking effect are specific and unexpected and so it is important to be able to break it when it occurs. Simplistically, you have to stop thinking. You need to get out of the situation where you are thinking about what you are doing. It is counter-intuitive as your brain will be trying to take over; in order to get better you need to concentrate more. This is wrong. Choking does not happen to everyone, because not everyone can choke. You have to be at the unconscious competence stage of what you are doing. You have to be very good at what you are doing. You cannot choke if you are mediocre.

Try this simple test; consider what you have to do to walk in a straight line. The movement sequence, the muscles that you use. Now really concentrate on how you walk in a straight line and imagine someone scrutinising how you do it. Now try to do it while still concentrating on how you are walking and you will find it starts to feel unnatural. This is for two reasons, one is that you are letting the conscious brain get involved and second you are now probably doing something that you would not normally because there are some things you do not even know you do, that your subconscious learned to do previously and that you have either forgotten or just never realised.

It can even affect something as simple as breathing. We all know how to breathe and we have been practising for years. We have achieved unconscious competence from a young age. Now, start focussing on your breathing and you will start to think about how often you are breathing, how deep you breathe in. You might even pause for a moment while you are thinking. It all suddenly starts to feel odd. You are thinking about something and consciously doing something that you wouldn't normally consider and because of that, you aren't as good at it. This is how choking works.

"Hard days are the best because that's when champions are made." - Gabby Douglas (1995-) Two-time Olympic Gold medallist in Artistic Gymnastics.

To develop a simple coping strategy, what would you normally think about before you choked when you were performing the same action? Let us say it is basketball and it is a free throw that you have suddenly become incapable of. To stop thinking about the throw, what would you normally think about? Maybe it is your positioning after the shot, about the next phase of the game once you have scored, where the person you are defending is going to go. It would be anything other than the throw so hone in on those thoughts and take the shot. A miss is a miss. It makes no logical sense that you 'suddenly' cannot make a shot you have been hitting for years. So you need to let it go if it happens and not think too much. What is happening is that both your chimp and your human are getting involved. To understand what this means, I need to introduce Steve Peters.

Exercising your Chimp

Dr Steve Peters is a Consultant Psychiatrist and University Senior Clinical Lecturer. Perhaps more importantly, and certainly for this book, Dr Steve Peters is one of the people behind the success of the GB Cycling team in the recent Olympics and Sky ProCycling team that recently won the Tour De France with Sir Bradley Wiggins among other victories. Multi-Olympic Medallists Victoria Pendleton CBE and Sir Chris Hoy strongly credit the work of Peters in their success.

What I am about to cover is a gross over-simplification of Dr Peters programme and I strongly recommend that all athletes should read his book rather than rely on my simple summary, but I hope that what I write here will interest you enough to do so. I always recommend that the athletes I coach read it and the successful ones do!

According to Peters' model, your brain is made up of a chimp, a human and a computer. The chimp is reactive and emotional, triggered by our animalistic, fight or flight preservation mode. Your computer is a storage and retrieval system for information and processes very quickly, without consideration or thought. It stores experiences and what Peters calls either autopilots or gremlins, depending on whether they are positive or negative. These computer 'routines' are simply preprogrammed reactions to situations that you have experienced before. It can be overridden by the human or the chimp because the routines aren't that strong, they are designed to be reprogrammed over time.

The human is the real you, the part that that thinks and considers, the rational part of your brain. Due to evolutionary needs, your brain has to work at different speeds. The computer is the fastest, reacting to a situation if it has a routine already. In other words, I've seen this before and this is how I react. This would be an unconscious operation. If the situation is new or different the chimp is the next fastest and also the strongest part of the brain because new and unusual situations can be dangerous, so the chimp assesses every situation in terms of survival. The chimp, although slower than the computer, reacts five times quicker than the human part and is also five times stronger, as its primary role is survival; it needs to be strong enough and fast enough to override everything else you might be thinking or doing. The human part of your brain is slower than the chimp, but this is because it takes the additional time to assess a situation and analyses the situation rationally, weighing options and selecting the appropriate response.

As I have explained previously, the normal operating level for someone at a high level in sport is unconscious competence. In Peter's model, achieving unconscious competence means that you have practiced the situation sufficiently that this is now locked into an autopilot routine in the computer part of your brain and you can now call it up quickly and unconsciously. In a stress or high pressure situation, the chimp senses danger, wakes up and takes control.

The chimp has very defensive, animalistic reactions to any situation. Its main purpose is survival, and so will try to avoid ‘dangerous’ situations. When you are coming up to a big competition and your internal voice is putting forward all the bad things that could happen, this is your chimp taking control, trying to get you to avoid the situation. Once the chimp is awake, your computer will not operate and the human part of your brain must consciously perform the operations.

Trying to ignore the chimp does not work, as the emotional feeling is five times stronger than your logical, human brain. To avoid choking, you cannot fight the chimp, you have to “exercise” it and allow it to calm down rather than trying to reason with it. You need to do this at a time that is suitable to you, and that is well before the competition. You need to show the chimp that you are not in any danger and that you have seen this situation before, that it is the same. To do this, rather than trying to suppress the feelings, you need to let them out for a time, let the chimp run wild, let your imagination conjure up all the things that you are worried about then deal with them.

In the week prior to a competition, spend 10 minutes each day where you let your chimp tell you all the things that will go wrong. What if you get an illness the day before an event? What if the competitors there are all better than you? What if you come last? What if you get injured? What if you embarrass yourself in front of the crowd and do something stupid?

Let the chimp get on with it for 10 minutes. Not only will it tire itself out, the doubts will become illogical. Once it has had its say, then it is time to put it in its cage and deal with the doubts logically. You are fit and healthy, you cannot control it if you pick up an illness but it is unlikely. You know how well prepared you are for this; you cannot control what the competition is. Someone has to come last and if it is you, you have ways of learning from this and it will help you move forward. Injuries happen, but they are unlikely. Crowds are not there to poke fun at people, they are there to support.

Once you have exercised the chimp and have considered its concerns logically, it will go back to sleep so you can continue with your preparation. You should repeat this cycle immediately prior to your event, just before your warm up. Once the chimp is asleep again, your human can sit back and let the computer do it's work, back to unconscious competence. If you find you do choke in the event, you deal with it the same way. Let your chimp run for a time and then deal with it. Because of your preparation, this should be quick enough that you can do this in a very short space of time, hopefully within the time you have available during the event.

Summary

Choking is every athlete's nightmare, but you can prevent it from becoming a debilitating issue. Knowing what it is, how it works, how to recognise it and how to overcome it will enable you to overcome a choke quickly and effectively if it ever happens to you.

1. Understand what choking is and do not get caught out.

2. Have a coping strategy.

3. Exercise your chimp

CHAPTER 21

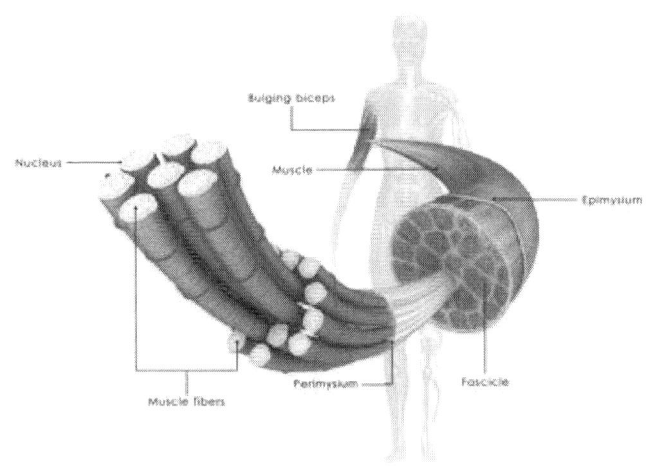

MANAGING INJURIES

Injuries are a fact of life. If you are playing any sport then, at some point, you are likely to pick up an injury. It may be a long term injury that needs significant rehabilitation, it might be a minor injury that happens at the worst possible time, or it might just be a minor injury with minor effects. The important element in all of these is how to manage yourself and your injury.

Damage control - The basics

The first thing to do is to stop using the injured area and start treatment as soon as possible. If the injury is serious then obviously a trip to the hospital straight away will start the ball rolling. For a less serious injury and if there is no first aid available, then a simple RICE (rest, ice, compression, elevation) protocol is usually a good start. However, the earliest you can take advice from a professional the better, even if it is on the phone.

- Rest – obviously stop using the part that is injured, take the weight off it or just immobilise it.

- Ice – get ice on it quickly to prevent the swelling that will slow the recovery. I always carry two or three of the instant ice packs. They are cheap and convenient. 10 minutes of applying ice (which will use two ice packs) is advised. Make sure you do not put ice on bare skin though as this can cause a nasty burn.

- Compression – depending on the injury, a compression bandage on the area or something similar will provide support and prevent further swelling.

- Elevation – get the injured part up in the air or up above the heart if possible. If that is a leg injury, then lying down with the leg elevated is good. Keeping the arm up in a sling if it is a wrist, or simply fastening a sleeve to the shoulder with a safety pin to hold the arm up is a good alternative. This keeps the blood flowing and prevents swelling again as the elevation helps the blood to return from the injured area.

So now that you have done your first steps, it is time to seek professional help. Many people believe that just resting a minor injury is sufficient and in some cases this will work. Often though, this can cause long term problems if this is the only treatment you have. Muscle tears will heal with rest but this will create scar tissue and when intense activities are resumed, the injury recurs. In sport your rehabilitation has two functions. First, it is to recover back to your previous level, and second, to do it as quickly as possible within the bounds of your injury. Resting on its own often achieves neither.

If you have a serious injury, get medial attention as soon as possible, either at Accident and Emergency or an early visit to a doctor. It is never too early to take professional advice. I have had an athlete pull a hamstring on a Sunday afternoon who was in discussion over the phone on the way home with their sport therapist and the rehabilitation commenced in the car. The serious rehabilitation started the next day with the first visit to the therapist. Sport Therapists are professional and so they obviously cost money. They are the most effective professionals to use for a sport injury, but if you cannot afford it, then go to your GP and, if possible, get referred to a physiotherapist. The difference between a Sport Therapist and a physiotherapist is that the latter is more general in nature whereas the former is much more specialist. Therefore a Sport Therapist will work on you to return you back to competition fitness in the most effective way, whereas a physiotherapist primarily works to remove the cause of the injury and return you back to normal health.

The medical response is the highest priority and once that is in progress, you must then start to manage the mental anguish that an injury causes. One way to understand your reactions to injury was written by Elizabeth Kubler Ross. There are a few different interpretations and this is by no means a definitive version, but it works for this instance.

Kubler Ross originally wrote about a person's response to being diagnosed as terminally ill. However, later research then showed that this process applied to many different traumatic events and an injury to a sportsman, especially one that is striving to become elite, is traumatic. While clearly this is not the same level of trauma that the model was written for, sports people will understand how this model works for them and, if you have been injured, you will recognise some of your responses to the injury.

Kubler Ross's cycle is not prescriptive, in that not everyone goes through every stage and the stages do not necessarily have a specific order. Generally though, the reactions and responses to an injury will resonate in roughly the order described here.

Shock

This is usually the first response; an initial shock that something serious has happened. Your body will start to process this quickly and the reaction will often be over very quickly. Usually the length of time this stage lasts (this is not medical shock) is dependent on how serious the injury is.

Denial

Often this will be the second response and it is important to understand that it is a very natural one. Everyone will initially go through it but you need to be overcome it quickly. You need to start to process the injury logically so you can make rational decisions on it before you do more damage. You will be unable to do this while you are in denial. Denial is your chimp taking control (See Chapter 18), because you are still in a competitive situation and you need to be able to continue to fight for your survival. “It’s not that bad”, “I can keep going” and “I can play on”. Sometimes, in the absence of a medical professional, a coach or parent has to step in to take responsibility for this, as usually they can be more objective than you. Sometimes, pure adrenaline can overcome the seriousness of the injury for a short time and you may not be in the best position to make the judgement.

The case described in Chapter 16 about the NFL rookie Robert Griffin III seems to be one of these, where the coach may wish he had taken control. As long as you understand that your initial reaction will be denial then you can overcome it and assess the extent of the injury. If you are trying to convince someone, yourself included, that you are okay or that the injury ‘isn’t as bad as it looks’ then take a deep breath and assess it rationally. Take your time, people will wait, there is no rush. If it hurts, you may think you can ‘run it off’. This is never the right thing to do. If it hurts, then that is your body’s way of telling you that something is wrong. Trying to run off the injury allows adrenaline to mask the pain but often results in further damage, lengthening the time it takes to recover.

If the injury is very acute then the denial may not be focussed on whether to play on, it might be about the seriousness of the injury. Simplistically, you need to get through denial and take a grip on the facts and start to work through the injury. As your priority is the medical response, you need to get through denial so this can start.

The next stages may happen in a random order to some extent and some may be repeated. They are often your chimp still taking control and you need to work through it and process each one.

Fear

Fear of the future is asking yourself (or others), will you ever be the same again? Is this a career threatening injury? If I miss training will I fall behind all my competitors? If I miss this opportunity will I get another one, or is this is my only chance? Fear is always about what might (or might not) happen. It is the unknown. Usually, this involves being scared of what could happen and assuming the worst. It is okay to voice your fears. Once you have laid them bare, you then need to process how likely each scenario is. Focus on getting facts. If you are scared of missing training, you need to find out how much training you are likely to miss and what the impact of missing that amount of train will be. Talk over your fears with someone that has experience or expert knowledge; an experienced athlete or coach, or a health professional.

You may well have new fears when it is time to return to full training. When I was 15 I broke my leg in seven places playing football. My return to training a year later was very difficult for me. Making the first tackle (which was how I broke my leg) took many failed attempts before I would allow myself to commit to it. You need to bring yourself back gradually, both for physical and psychological reasons. You need to progressively test your body as well as build your confidence.

Anger

You may be angry with yourself, for getting in a situation that caused the injury. You may be angry with your coach, your parents, or the opponent who injured you. You might even be angry with the people who are telling you the prognosis, especially if you are still in denial. There are many people to be angry with and you cannot cope with it merely by trying to suppress it. You need to vent some, to get it out of your system, to allow your chimp to exercise so it can go back to sleep. This is the same principle as how you would to deal with a choking situation as described in Chapter 18. But you also need to be careful not to hit out at the people who are helping you or, if you do, recognise it for what it is and apologise quickly and sincerely.

Guilt

You may feel that you have let your team down becausc they were relying on you. You have let your coach down who has put so much effort into getting you where you are. You have let your parents down who have supported you for so long. You have even let yourself down. You didn't prepare properly, you made a stupid mistake. You should not have gone into that tackle.

None of this is true and it is again your chimp (see Chapter 18) taking control. No-one wants to be injured, no-one plans on it. There is no-one (who matters) that will blame you other than yourself. Try apologising for getting injured and see what reaction you will get. Let your chimp run riot for a while with all the reasons why you have let everyone down and you will come up with all the reasons I have covered above and a few more. Once you have done that and started to run out of the reasons why you feel guilty, start to look at it logically. If one of your team-mates gets injured, do you get angry at them? Are your parents angry or disappointed in you or are they just worried about you? That only really leaves your feelings about yourself. If you made a mistake, deal with it like you would poor performance as I showed you in Chapter 17.

Grief

Often the most overwhelming emotion in an injury is the sense of loss; lost opportunity, loss of ability, lost time. It is a sadness that may only be an underlying feeling but it will be a pervading one while you are injured and sometimes afterwards. This is usually the lowest point for anyone in this cycle. The most important element here is to understand that this is a natural feeling. You have experienced a traumatic event. The problem for many is that non-athletes do not understand the level of psychological trauma involved. They can write off your grief as trivial. It is only sport, it is not that important. You will be okay. This can be confusing because your feelings do not match what they are saying. It is much more traumatic to you as you feel you have (temporarily) lost the most important thing in your life.

Recovery

Now that you are in the process and you can understand your reactions to the injury, you can start to mentally recover. Recovery comes from dealing with the injury and the time that you are injured. Kubler Ross described the next stages as Understanding, Acceptance and Integration.

Understanding is exactly what has been described in the first stages. If you understand that they exist, that they are natural and what they are, then you are in a better position to achieve acceptance and move forward to integration. This means that you integrate the injury into your development program. It has happened, now you must make the best of it.

Moving Forward

"Work hard and have patience. Because no matter who you are, you're going to get hurt in your career and you have to be patient to get through the injuries." Randy Johnson, former US Baseball player (1963-present)

First, you need to assess how long you will be out of normal action; a week, a month, a year. Be realistic as it is important for the next stages.

Once you are clear on the amount of time you are going to adapt for, then you can start assessing what your adaptation needs to be for this period. You need to find out, based on advice, what you can and cannot do. If you injured a lower limb, an ankle for example, can you work on your core or your upper body (or both)? If it is only one ankle, can you do single leg work? If you have injured your dominant leg, this could be a great time to work on your weaker leg. Maybe, some additional flexibility work on other parts of your body are possible, or doing low impact work, like Tai-Chi. Working on balance or isometric holds can also be very beneficial. You might have to be creative and more holistic in your approach to your training, but, on the other hand, this could be an opportunity to strengthen the areas that you do not normally have time to work on.

Additionally, there are all the other things that you do not get time to do when they are training that they can work on while they are injured. One example is to watch your sport. Sometimes, competitors do not get to watch much of their own sport. If you are a footballer, watch some matches. Watch teams that are better than yours, or older. Watch your own team, watch your competition. Do not just watch, though, watch with a critical eye. What works and what does not work? What are their strengths and weaknesses as a team? What do the individual players do that you could learn from? There is plenty to be taken from watching. It might be on TV or it might be video on YouTube, but there is plenty out there that you can learn from if you watch properly. Believe it or not, in some cases like tennis or football watching properly can contribute to your 10,000 hours as this helps to develop your sport-specific visual acuity.

Other than watching, you can also brush up on your knowledge. Find out what is new in your sport, what people are doing that you are not. Check whether there are any new autobiographies released, or ones that you may have missed that you can read. Catch up on the reports and magazine articles that you never have the time to read. Repeat all the things that you did after Chapter 2, and bring yourself up to date or just update your knowledge based on where you are now.

Lastly you can refine your plan going forward for once you are injury free. Your schedule is now likely be different to what your coach was working on and if you are part of a team or a training group, your schedule is now different to theirs as you come back to full capability. Work with your coach to plan what you will be doing, in training and your competition schedule. Get into some detail. A 400m Hurdler who wants to run in an Olympic final can find details that they need to be working on. What are the qualifying times to make the Olympic A and B standards and what are the people who do qualify running in the competition? How do they run their race, what are their touch-down times off each hurdle, their overall times, time to first hurdle, time from last hurdle to finish, time from hurdle 8 to finish, time from hurdle 1 to hurdle 9? All of these will inform your training and development. All of which you will not have time to work out in normal circumstances. You will be able to create your own examples from your own sport.

Injury is not a great time for anyone and none of us would plan to take time out to work on the things I have outlined above. However, these things happen and it is important not only to limit the damage but to come back strong. It would be churlish to think that you can return stronger, but you may be able to improve on some things that you may otherwise have been deficient in. Using my own example again, while I was working on my rehabilitation I spent a long time training my very weak left leg by kicking left footed, even though I was a completely right-footer player. In the end, I became 'naturally' two footed (you know from earlier chapters that there is no such thing as natural talent). But I could kick just as well with either foot. This is something I would never have managed had I not been forced to by injury and I was probably a better player for it as a result.

Summary

With injuries you have to be patient to recover and not come back too quickly. In order to be patient, you must be working on things that will maintain your development, albeit in a more general, less specific way. You cannot afford to take it easy with this work because you will not fool yourself. You must commit yourself in the same way as you would normally train. It does matter and it is important, so approach it in the same way that you would approach any level of training and development.

1. Understand the stages you will go through and accept them – Shock, Denial, Fear, Anger, Guilt, Grief, Acceptance and Adaptation.

2. Assess the time you have for your adapted programme.

3. Plan what you can do physically based on your injury limitations and work on them.

4. Watch and learn.

5. Improve your knowledge.

6. Plan your comeback.

CHAPTER 22

LUCK IS FOR LEPRECHAUNS

"Luck is for leprechauns and you're not green"
Eric Thomas (present) Renowned motivational speaker and author

Science and Superstition

This statement by Eric Thomas sums up my views on luck and superstition. This chapter will not be for everyone. If you believe in luck, if you have superstitions that you are happy with, and even if you believe in a higher power to help you then this chapter may not resonate for you. I believe that subscribing to luck as a reason for anything happening is devolving yourself of responsibility for things that happen. If you do that, then you might as well invest in more charms than training and practice.

"The harder I work the luckier I get" Nick Faldo (1957-) English former World No.1 Golfer

"The more I practice the luckier I get" Jerry Barber (1916-1994) US Golfer

Sport is about many things, but it is not about luck or superstition. Sometimes, things do not go your way and sometimes they do. A poor cup draw that pools you against the best team in the first round, a poor decision that goes against you, the ball that does not quite fall the way you want it to. These are the kind of things we ascribe to as luck.

Yet when the ball goes the way we want it to, it is all too often not due to good luck, instead it is our ability or skill. If we want the ball to go a certain way and it does, then that is obviously down to our skill, if it does not, it is bad luck. Think how ridiculous that sounds. The luck fairy only intervenes in a bad way. We only have bad luck; we do not really have good luck. Sure, we might get a bye occasionally and that would be good luck, but generally, we only apply luck to things that do not go our way. Alternatively, other people attribute the things that we do to good luck, usually to our own disgust.

Luck versus probability

Sport is generally pure (cheating aside) in that the best team or best player usually wins. There might be occasions when the underdogs win, but that is because they have been better on the day. 'Luck' balances out over time, because it is a direct function of the player or team's ability. To assign good luck to someone's performance, or your own, belittles the effort and sweat that the player has put into getting to this point. To attribute bad luck to something is an abdication of responsibility for the performance.

"Confidence is what happens when you've done the hard work that entitles you to succeed." - Pat Summitt, former US women's college basketball coach. (Present)

If you are relying on luck to pull you through, then you have probably run out of talent. Sometimes you might attempt a shot that comes off that usually would not. Sometimes your opponent attempts a shot that usually would and it does not. T his is probability, not luck. It might become the turning point of a match, but it only does so when you react in such a way that means it is, when you apply a level of importance to it. However, that does not change the probability of whether it might happen or not.

The probability of a shot coming off is only improved by how well you know how to play it, how practised you are. You might pull off the occasional 'lucky' shot but that is only because conditions have favoured you in one particular set of circumstances, which is why you will probably not repeat it. The more variables there are, the less repeatable the activity.

Why is it important to understand that luck does not exist? First, as stated previously, attributing a performance to good luck does not recognise that it is the outcome of hard work and practice. Therefore it means that you are not recognising that hard work and practice leads to a higher level of performance. Second, and more usual, is that assigning a loss or a poor performance to bad luck does not lead to any improvement. You know how to deal with poor performance from Chapter 17 but if we do not see it as poor performance, merely bad luck, then there is no reason to analyse the performance. You cannot analyse luck, it is just something that happens that you have no control over. Therefore the obvious route will be to 'hope' for better luck next time. It is a platitude, to yourself or by someone else.

The 'Lucky Pants'

Belief in superstition is worse than belief in luck. This is because superstition is inevitably debilitating. It defies all logic and once logic is lost, then superstition can spiral out of control. Before I get into superstition it is worth ruling out some things that are seen as superstitions but are actually just good practice; following a fixed routine in the preparation for the race, wearing the same shoes, the same outfit. This makes sense. It is a routine you are comfortable with. It is part of your preparation (see Chapter 11). It can be taken to a very high level. Cycling's Team Sky leaves nothing to chance and have a team that goes ahead of the riders and completely strips the hotel rooms, replaces the mattresses, bed linen and even the air conditioning units in the rooms. This ensures that when the riders return to the hotel (which is different to the one they left that morning) there is a level of consistency. If it was someone saying "I have to have the same sheets every night" this could be seen to be a superstition. When Team Sky takes that to a logical extreme, then it is controlling variables.

The important way to differentiate between superstition and consistent preparation is the principle of causality. There is a direct link between how well someone sleeps and relaxes and their performance. There is no causality between someone touching the grass of the field with their right hand before they take to the pitch and their performance. The first is preparation, the second is superstition.

How do superstitions arise in sports people? Again, it comes back to causality, but with a superstition, it is when a sportsman or sportswoman applies causality where none exists. When some element is slightly different from the norm (such as different underwear because the regular set has been forgotten) and the performance goes well, the player illogically applies causality to the underwear, their 'lucky pants'. The player then believes that the underwear has an impact on his/her performance.

Where this starts to break down is when the player starts to believe that without that set of underwear they will perform badly. Unfortunately this then becomes self-fulfilling. The psychological principle of confirmation bias has two aspects. The first is illusory correlation, when you believe a false correlation between two events, like the belief that the lucky pants make you play better. When the player takes to the field with his new superstition intact he plays with confidence and his reinforces his belief. The second is belief perseverance, when a belief persists even when evidence shows it to be false, such as if the performance is not as good, then this will not break the superstition, rather the performance will be attributed to something else.

If, for whatever reason, the superstition is not fulfilled, the lucky pants have been accidentally left at home, the player will **expect** to play badly. We create the reality we expect so a poor performance is therefore inevitable, further reinforcing the illusory correlation and entrenching the superstition. Social psychology calls this cognitive dissonance where people enhance evidence that support their opinions and reduce evidence that contravenes it. It was actually first coined by a psychologist called Leon Festinger in 1956 during a study of followers of a UFO cult based on how they would rationalise their beliefs.

Once a superstition takes hold, eventually, other superstitions will arise as other unusual situations occur and the player assigns causality which can eventually lead to the situation where the player has half a dozen superstitions, all of which he or she believes affect their performance. The reason this is so debilitating is that if any one of these superstitions is not in place for any reason, the player will unreasonably and illogically perform badly.

The superiority of science

The simple fact is that sport is based on science; physics, biochemistry, biomechanics and many other disciplines, all of which are scientific. Whether or not you learn the science behind your sport, you have someone else to advise you or you just learn from experience of what works and what does not, it is all science. The more you practice, the more your body learns to perform specific movements quicker and more accurately. The more the computer in your head recognises situations and acts and responds to them without conscious thought, the better you will be. It is that simple. It is romantic to believe that some external influence plays a part and it is less romantic to believe it all comes down to repetitive practice and sweat, but science will beat romance every time.

"Obsessed is just a word that the lazy use to describe the dedicated" – Russell Warren (1971-) English Cricketer

Faith is slightly different. Faith can motivate you, but, no matter which God you believe in, there is no reason why you would be favoured over another athlete who believes in his or her own God. No-one gets handed anything just by praying for it. It may be your religion that gives you your motivation and drives you on, but it does not give you the skill that you need; only practice can do that.

Summary

Luck and superstition have no place in sport. Put your sporting faith in science, in training and in your preparation. They are the only things that will affect your performance positively.

1. Identify practices that are causal to good preparation and those which may be superstitions

2. Logically analyse the superstitions to confirm what they are.

3. Discard the superstitions.

CHAPTER 23

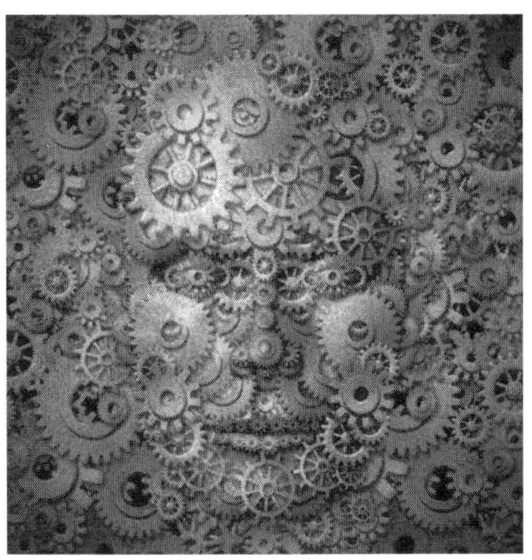

BRINGING IT ALL TOGETHER

If you want to attain an elite level in sport, there will be obstacles. Many, many obstacles. But those obstacles are there no matter who you are and you have to resolve to overcome them all. There will be many people who will tell you that you can't do it. One of those people will be yourself.

If you start to listen to those people (or if you doubt yourself), ask yourself if you have proven beyond any doubt that you cannot do it. I will repeat the principle of Carl Cantrell from Chapter 9. We don't even know enough about the function of the human body and mind as an athlete to be able to prove that any individual person cannot achieve their desired goals. Have you exhausted every possible option to get where you want to be? Have you tried everything that you can think of and everything that everybody else has tried?

There are no guarantees. But, until you have tried everything, you just don't know. In this chapter I'm going to summarise the action steps that I gave you in each previous chapter so you can see how they fit together. If you do all of this and still don't make it, then at least you can look back and say that you gave it your best shot. But one thing I will guarantee is that you will have got a lot further than you would have if you hadn't done them.

Step by Step

Start with a dream and define it properly. Identify what it is you want to achieve, keeping it simple. It should be out of reach but not out of sight; it needs to be stretching, almost beyond what you think is possible.

Write your dream down. Make it real by speaking it into existence.

Stick what you have written down somewhere you can spend time with it. The bathroom door, your bedroom, in your locker.

Make your dream live in your mind. Fill it with sights, sounds, smells and feelings.

Identify who will support you. Be realistic about what you expect from them and choose wisely.

Share your dream. Get the support for your journey and support others in theirs.

Learn the rules of your sport. Know how they work and how they are applied.

Learn the sport. Get a deep understanding of how the sport is played at an elite level.

Learn the governance and structure, who is responsible for what, who makes the rules and limitations for where you compete.

Try things out! Be prepared to have a go and push the boundaries of how the game is played, but do it when the competition doesn't matter.

Find people in sport who inspire you or whose achievements you want to emulate (it does not have to be in your own sport)

Read about them, watch or listen to interviews, read their autobiography, learn from them.

Look at how they got to the top, what they are doing, how committed they are and were.

Apply what you have learned to your own approach. What are the things that they did or do that you aren't doing? Are there things that you could be doing more of, less of, or differently?

Create 'Brand You' and be the brand. How you act is how people perceive you and for them, their perception is reality. You need to make sure the perceptions people have of you are the ones you want them to have.

Actively network with people. Make contacts and cultivate them. Seek out opportunities that will put you in contact with people who you can network with.

Be cheeky, do not be shy about talking about needing support, but do not just outright and ask for sponsorship in the very first conversation with someone. Build a relationship.

Develop skills you might need, take opportunities to learn. This could be from school, college or just learning informally from someone else.

Use your social networking skills for positive networking and promotion.

Create a blog or other promotional site. Put positive messages on there, use it to promote the 'Brand You'.

What's your why? Find your intrinsic motivation and enhance it.

Create 7 time clock faces in ½ hour intervals, one for each day of the week.

Fill in your sleep, work/school and training times. Be clear on what you actually do, don't pad it if you don't do it.

Identify your leisure time and what you do in it. This includes time on the phone, watching TV and simple gaps in your schedule where you aren't doing something 'constructive'.

If you have a conflict or dilemma that means you have to make a sacrifice, write it out as described in Chapter 6, including all the 'Because' statements. Use the style shown in the book or download a template from www.newpersonalbest.co.uk/book

Review the 'Because' statements to see if you can evaporate the cloud and fulfil both needs. Are all the assumptions you have made in the 'Because' statements correct and unchangeable.

Adjust your perspective, see things from others point of view. Are you wanting too much or being selfish?

Adjust your timeframe, take a longer term view. Can the things that you think you are sacrificing now be delayed in the short, medium or long term rather than simply sacrificed?

Throw off the duvet. Take that first step, whatever it might be.

Stop planning and start moving.

Don't 'do', pursue. Stop doing your sport and pursue your dream.

Take responsibility both for the things you do and for the things that 'happen to you'. Take control of your life.

Read at least one of the recommended books so you understand the importance of proper, purposeful practice.

Overcome your circumstances. There are obstacles, but nothing is insurmountable.

Use what you do have to your advantage.

Play the long game. Do not sweat being a mid-table competitor at a young age. It is the end result that matters.

Look at elite athletes in your sport and outside your sport and identify what they are doing differently to you and write them down.

Be objective in why you are not doing those things (remember though that some things can not be sacrificed; i.e. education or health)

Introduce the appropriate parts from your list into your training – number of times per week, conditioning, nutrition, flexibility, recovery, and hydration.

Be aware of your training load and keep your coach informed of the other things you are doing.

Warm up correctly.

Avoid fatigue.

Learn the correct techniques for every movement.

Stretch.

Practise a pre-competition routine and stick to it (do not introduce anything new in a competition phase, such as new food).

If your competition schedule is irregular or intermittent (as opposed to playing matches every week) then understand how tapers work and practise them.

Practise your feeding routine and stick to it.

Hydrate properly for a week ahead of a big competition (or preferably take care of your hydration all the time!)

Get plenty of rest in the week before a competition, especially if you are prone to sleeplessness the night before.

Keep your hands clean!

Manage your competition mental state by practising how you want to feel and anchoring the feeling to a physical action so you call up this mental state at any time.

Practice getting into the zone so you can play every game at the peak of your performance level.

Identify your constraint, use the 80/20 rule to work out where you can gain the most benefit.

Exploit your constraint. Get absolutely everything out of the constraint that you can.

Subordinate everything else to your constraint. Make sure your decisions make allowance for the constraint, don't expose it.

Elevate your constraint, get better at what is limiting you.

When you have a new constraint, apply the rules to the new one and start the five step process again.

Develop a growth mindset

Modify your language in terms of praise, of yourself and of others.

Focus on the learning and the challenge, not the outcome or the achievement

Find a team, club or training group that is better than you are.

Strive to learn everything you can from that training group.

Become the best of that training group.

Find another training group that is better than you are.

Compete, do not just win.

Take an occasional checkpoint of progress by competing at your own level.

Be aware of mental techniques and especially the ones that your competitors can and will use against you.

Actively manage your 'ambience', what you display to your competition.

Model the behaviour of how you want to be perceived.

Practice the modelling.

Identify a 'rough-cut' route to get to your dream, with the things you have identified you want to achieve along the way

Write down the approximate timing along the way.

Add a 'tolerance' to the timings – be pragmatic and make it as wide as possible – plus or minus a year for example.

Now add a fallback – if not that event, then what are the others that you can target within your tolerance band?

Be realistic – how important are the targets to the end goal? Are they 'nice to have' because they are good indicators for you personally, or is it genuinely impossible to get to the next stage without completing this one?

If you are a younger athlete your development will slow down at some point. Be prepared for it.

Be aware of the advantages your development age has on you and work with it, do not rely on it or be overwhelmed by it.

Write your lists, improve what you can improve and discard the things you have no control over.

Understand what choking is, and do not get caught out.

Have a coping strategy. Prepare it, develop it and recognise when to implement it.

Exercise your chimp. Do it routinely whether you are feeling nervous or not, don't let your chimp catch you unawares.

Understand the stages you will go through if you get injured and accept them – Shock, Denial, Fear, Anger, Guilt, Grief, Acceptance and Adaptation.

If you get injured, assess the time you have for your adapted programme.

Plan what you can do physically based on your injury limitations and work on them.

If you're out of action, take the time to watch and learn.

Improve your knowledge.

Plan your comeback.

Identify practices that are causal to good preparation and those which may be superstitions.

Logically analyse the superstitions to confirm what they are.

Discard the superstitions – with confidence.

Last and most important, go out and be all that you can be.

You can find templates for the 'Evaporating Cloud' and the 'Clock Face' at newpersonalbest.co.uk/book and there you will also find a link to my forum where you are welcome to ask questions, post comments or just hang out.

Appendices

Appendix 1 – Training Theory

There is something very important that you need to understand about training; it does not make you stronger. If it is done correctly it will cause just the right amount of damage. What actually makes you stronger is your body's reaction to training, the recovery. This means that recovery is just as important, if not more important, than the training. You cannot have one without the other. To understand the importance of recovery and how it can be maximised, it is worth understanding the background at a molecular level of how your body functions in terms of rest and recovery.

The 'training effect' principle is the basis of all scientific training programmes in any sport. This principle basically states that when a muscle cell is subjected to physical exertion, molecular damage will occur. The human body is programmed to rebuild the cell to a slightly higher level to prevent damage from the same level of exercise in future. Improvement takes so long because you are changing your body a few molecules and cells at a time. It takes a lot of these small changes to make a noticeable effect.

It takes time for your body to rebuild the cells from the damage caused. To improve the amount of time that it takes, requires active recovery so that your body is assisted in every way possible to accelerate the process. However, you should be aware that the time taken can be significantly affected by other processes that your body is carrying out, such as fighting an illness (which is an excellent reason why you should not train when you are ill). This is also why alcohol (and the hangover that goes with it) and training don't mix. Your body prioritises its recovery. If you are fighting an illness, you won't be recovering minor muscle damage. The same goes if you have a hangover and then train.

Once the cells have finished rebuilding, your body will maintain this new molecular structure for 24-36 hours while it awaits the activity to occur again at the same intensity. If this doesn't happen, then it will begin to atrophy (breaking down again to a lower molecular level to conserve energy - a survival mechanism from the hunter-gatherer era). When training ceases, the training effect will also stop. It gradually reduces at approximately one third of the rate of acquisition (Jenson and Fisher, 1972).

Training effect curves (Figure 1)

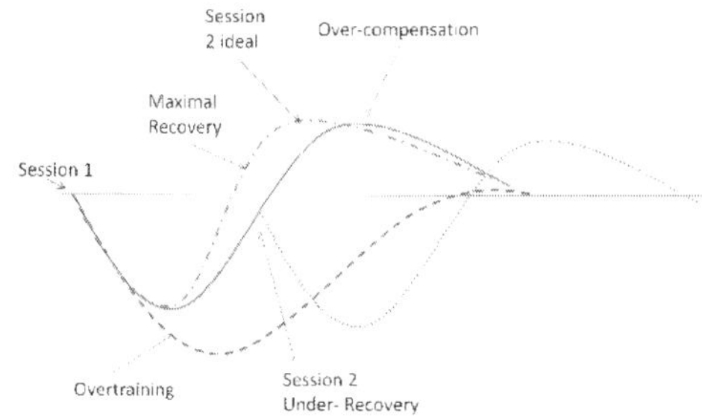

A regular training effect curve can be seen above in Figure 1 as a solid line. The flat line represents a steady state. During a training session, identified as Session 1, the molecular damage is shown as a dip. Once the session (and the damage) finishes, then the body starts to rebuild beyond the original steady state and this is called over-compensation or super-compensation. After a time the atrophy begins and eventually the body will return to its steady state.

Maximising Recovery

Where does recovery sit in terms of importance to you? Often, recovery is just the period between one session and the next. It may be a simple case of rest and relaxation. However, you can accelerate recovery which will then mean that either you can do more sessions (notwithstanding specific recovery requirements for high intensity sessions that affect the central nervous system) or that the sessions can be more effective. As shown in

Figure 1, the point at which you can commence session 2 is earlier.

Before and During Training.

Recovery starts before training. You have to be fully prepared for training and at 100% fitness, otherwise the starting point of the dip is too low and you will suffer from overtraining (see later). This means that you need to be properly fuelled, properly hydrated, and recovered from the previous session. One thing to be careful of is that coaches who have lots of athletes to look after (which is most of us), will assume during training planning that recovery takes place based on general principles such as separating CNS sessions and high intensity sessions and pairing strength session with particular track sessions etc. However, if the you have been undertaking a physically demanding job during the day or have done a 5K cross country run at school this may not be picked up and can also cause overtraining.

Staying hydrated is essential as well as staying fuelled if the session is particularly long. Energy drinks, energy gels, flapjacks, and bananas can all help here.

Post training

This is when the work on recovery really starts. Your body reacts quickly and has some golden times as follows;

Immediately on finishing.

Drink 250ml of energy drink and top up your glycogen levels. My athletes love the fact that I advise them to eat jelly sweets. There are some very good all-natural and organic jelly sweets around, or some sports drinks manufacturers also manufacture special sweets. This should be done in the first 60 seconds.

The first half an hour.

This is where the body is in an anabolic state doing the maximum it can to recover as quickly as possible. As can be seen from Figure 1, recovery is exponential so this is the point where the most can be achieved.

- Take on more carbohydrates (another 250ml of energy drink as a starting point)
- Take in protein for muscle regeneration.
- Take on any ergogenic supplements, such as vitamins, that you feel are appropriate.
- Ice down any problem areas.
- Do a cool down appropriate to the session.

Here are some examples:

Have a couple of apples, washed down by a sport drink followed by some cheese.

Have a large chocolate milk shake, or if you want to be a bit more specific;

Have a sport drink, then, have a protein drink with additional Glutamine. Also take on a multi vitamin, glucosamine, chlondroitin and cod liver oil.

Up to 2 hours.

Once you have cooled down a little this is the time to stretch. Do a general stretch of all areas but pay particular attention to the areas that have had the most work. Stretching should be deep and held for 30 seconds each. No bouncing. This stretch is to realign all the muscle fibres that have suffered from micro-damage. Stretch opposing muscles in pairs (such as stretching quads then hamstrings) not in a random order. Start stretching from the core outwards.

Hydrotherapy helps flush the toxins from the muscles by causing the blood to flow back and forth in a greater quantity. This can be done simply by turning the shower hot and cold or switching between a hot shower and a cold bath a few times. For best effect the body must be given time to react and therefore a couple of minutes each is necessary. Alternately, take a cool bath. This is not the same as an ice-bath, which is becoming popular in sport. Recent research published in the European Journal of Applied Physiology has found that ice baths are useful during intense competition, but actually offer no benefit in regular recovery. In some cases they can actually reduce training benefit by inhibiting the recovery process.

Towards the end of the 2 hours, eat a small meal with some carbohydrates and protein.

Post 2 hours.

Rest and relax, preferably sleep.

Training and recovery have a symbiotic relationship and it is important to understand that without recovery, training adaptations do not take place. Obviously recovery will happen naturally, but what you should try to achieve is the maximum recovery in the shortest possible time. This is shown on the diagram as the dotted line titled Maximal Recovery.

In the same way that you should not leave training to chance, recovery shouldn't be left to chance either. Training is only 100% effective if your body is prepared for it. What this 'preparation' entails varies but for your purposes this means that you are not approaching training in any way depleted. (Adenosine Triphosphate)

Hydration

This is the easiest of easy wins. Proper hydration is so uncommon in many athletes. Normal guidelines issued by health services must be seen only as a minimum by you as an athlete because they are based on low activity levels. Government guidelines for water intake recommend 6-8 glasses of water per day. An athlete intensively training for 2 hours in normal conditions needs to be far better hydrated than an average normal person. Just a 2% of bodyweight loss through dehydration is detrimental to your performance and will result in fatigue. If an athlete commences training at this level the session is worse than useless. Staying hydrated is vital all week long irrespective of a hydration plan for training itself. For a run of the mill, daytime hydration strategy a combination of regular intakes of water helps and you can get a double benefit from taking on 'wet-carbohydrate' type fruits such as oranges, but keep a track of where you are otherwise you will fail to stay hydrated. There are a variety of ways to do this such as a glass of water every hour, having a drink bottle that you sip from over the course of a morning so you know how much you have (or haven't!) taken. A simple indicator is that urine should be the colour of light straw, if you are any darker then you are dehydrated.

Before exercise is when sports drinks come into play. These enable you to process the liquid better and also add in electrolytes and other elements that you will need. Start with 500ml in the half-hour before exercise. This tops off your hydration levels and gives you a start for the session.

During the session, your body will consume liquid and sweat it out. One way of finding out how much fluid is lost during a session is to weigh in before and after. 1Kg of bodyweight lost is equal to 1000ml of fluid. If any fluid is taken during the session then this needs to be factored in as well.

Fluid Loss = (Body Weight before) - (Body Weight After) + drink volume during.

As an Example, an athlete training for 2 hours on a warm day, weighs 90kg before and 88Kg after + 500ml during = 1500ml lost (1Kg = 1000ml)

In our example above, our athlete would need to consume 1500ml of liquid to maintain hydration levels over the course of a session but this should be taken in small amounts to avoid over-hydration e.g. 250ml maximum every 15 minutes. Bringing this into practical terms, that is equivalent to a 500ml bottle of sports drink every 30 minutes, or 3 during a 90 minute session. How many athletes do you know that bring a six-pack for one 2-hour session (including before and after).

The above is just a guideline but shows how far out a lot of athlete's hydration management can be. Clearly, weather conditions and the type of session as well as the individual's metabolism will vary but to get the absolute maximum benefit from a training session this needs to be taken seriously.

Diet

Most athletes have reasonably healthy diets. Again, however, normal guidelines do not take into account the requirements of an athlete. There are different theories over what is and is not required and this chapter is not designed to analyse all the research.

Most athletes do not take on enough protein. A portion of protein should be part of every meal including (and especially) breakfast. While carbohydrates are the most important aspect of fuel for an athlete, because their protein intake is usually inadequate it is the highest priority on my list. The main reason protein intake is low tends to be because athletes assume it is meat or fish and this is only a main meal intake. However, peanut butter, baked beans, cheese rolls, yoghurt and eggs are also all good sources of protein. As an example a 90Kg athlete will need greater than 120g of protein per day.

Carbohydrates are the single most important fuel for athletes but the advantage is that there are lots of sources of carbohydrates and even your sports drinks contribute. Pasta is a good staple and potatoes and bread weigh in quite nicely too. Fruit is also a good source of carbohydrate. However, you need a lot. For an average athlete of 90Kg a rough guide would be a requirement of 900g of carbohydrate intake per day (source UKA).

Leaving aside supplements, a good way of keeping on top of micro-nutrient intake is to eat lots of fresh fruit and vegetables. While government guidelines recommend for a normal person is 5 portions of fruit or vegetables per day for an athlete (and recent studies have shown that for normal people as well) 7-8 portions per day are required. Fruit smoothies are a fantastic source of a few portions in one go.

Bringing together the information above and putting it into action is not as complicated as it sounds if a simple plan is followed:

- Eat smaller meals more regularly than an average person would; every 2 hours is better than a couple of big meals per day. Think of it this way, if you had built a fire and wanted to keep it fuelled, you would not build it right up with logs to get a roaring fire and then let it burn completely down to embers before building it right up again and repeating the cycle. This is effectively what you are doing with a two meals a day approach. You overeat your food at the set mealtime, beyond what your body can process and then you let the fuel element of the meal burn away until you are hungry at which point you over-feed again. The hunger is the point when the fire has almost gone out. The way you fuel a fire is once it is built up, you let it burn down a little then add another log to keep it going. Adding smaller amounts of fuel more regularly keeps the fire at an even level, so have a breakfast in the morning and then top it off every couple of hours. Have smaller amounts of fuel but more regularly.

- Eat protein with every meal. Most athletes do not get enough protein. Muscle repair after training requires protein, as stated earlier. But repair is not just about the initial recovery, it is an ongoing process and maintaining sufficient protein in meals is important. Protein shakes are a good supplement for post training, but other 'complete' (containing all the essential amino acids) protein sources include dairy products, like milk and yoghurt, eggs, fish, meat and mixes of grains, beans, nuts and seeds.

- Have carbohydrate with each meal and include wet carbohydrates such as juicy fruit (not the sweets!) where possible.

This will keep you on top of your intake for carbohydrates, protein and nutrients without getting bloated. Also, this will cover a further point for training itself, in that you should not eat too close to training but you should be well fuelled. Your last meal should be 2 hours before training, but topped off with a snack like an energy bar, flapjack or fruit 45-30 minutes before. If the training session is a long one you may need to snack again during the session.

Appendix 2 - Female Athletes

To be successful in sport, there are some fundamental requirements that are usually present. I have covered the requirement to be self-disciplined, focused and having a burning desire to succeed in other chapters in the book. The other things that are required are self-confidence and competitiveness, which is a form of aggression. You have to want to beat people and break your own limits.

Generally however, while women can have an abundance of self discipline and focus, men have, on average, higher self-esteem than women and are also more aggressive from a very early age (Scientific American April 2001 by Roy F Baumeister).

As with everything previously written in this book, the best way to overcome the obstacles is to be aware of them and understand them. With women and girls, the barriers to sport are greater than for men, with participation and opportunity lower. Such barriers start at a young age where sport is seen as masculine and elitist culturally. In most cultures, especially in the west, women are not raised to be competitive. Their body should not be muscular as this is seen as 'manly'. There are also generally fewer opportunities to participate with fewer sports clubs geared to women or less teams.

Simplistically, girls and women follow the same 10,000 hour rule as boys, but because of their 'play' during their early years tend to develop fundamental movement skills later. Seemingly, 'simple' movements such as running, throwing and catching are generally not done as much at a younger age as with boys and this can significantly affect self-confidence in sporting endeavours, especially as the ability gap widens.

Additionally, according to the Canadian Association for Advancement of Women's Sport, the "challenge of competition" is a significant negative factor for women and this is undesirable for them. They have found that some women and girls feel that competition can jeopardize relationships as someone can be hurt emotionally (by defeat or poor performance, non-selection) or physically. A much higher proportion of women than men participate in non-competitive exercise rather than competitive sport.

Self-esteem issues in women and girls and lack of confidence can greatly affect athletics development. The approach described in Chapter 14 is far easier for a man or boy to implement than for a girl or woman who may have much lower self-confidence or self-esteem. In this instance, however, it can be easier for a girl to progress if she mentally approaches the challenge differently. Whereas males will reach the top of their training group and then need to move on, in many cases females who reach the top relative to their female peers can simply compete with the males to drive them on and remain within the same training group.

This gives greater scope for choosing competitive training partners to pull you along. Therefore, through athletic development and a change of mindset (coupled with a flexible coach) will allow most girls the opportunity to always be competing against someone better than them within their training group.

The difficulty comes with the competitive mindset that allows this to happen. This is something that females must expend much more energy on than men in general. To be come successful you must place an emphasis on this element of your development. In Chapter 12 on mental preparation, there is a technique for triggering the frame of mind you wish to be in. For women, one of these is self-confidence and competitiveness, and if you're a woman I recommend that you have anchors for both states of mind, which you use in **every training session,** not just for competition. You need to practice being in that state of mind all the time that you are performing your sport. If you cannot do it in training with people around you that you know, you will not be able to do it in competition in a higher-pressure environment.

If you particularly suffer from nerves or anxiety in competition then you really must address this. Simply competing and hoping for the best is not going to resolve the issue and it will have a huge impact on your performance level. I cannot stress enough the impact of nerves and pre-competitive stress. This impacts your energy levels by increasing your heart rate and the amount of adrenaline for prolonged periods which saps the body of energy. It will also inevitably move you into the conscious competence mode which is not the level you should be performing at. If you cannot relax sufficiently you will not perform to your maximum capability when it matters. If you really suffer, you may need to consider being very careful at what level you compete at. With boys I am usually happy throwing them in a high level and then slowly reeling that level in with regards to performance. I would not do that with my female athletes as they generally need to be much closer in terms of performance to what they are chasing, otherwise they can lose motivation.

Another issue that affects girls, more so than women and certainly more than boys, is body image. According to research undertaken by MIND in 2012, women battle with body confidence issues when participating in outdoor exercise and as a consequence many prefer loose or baggy clothing when exercising. Competition clothing and team kit has a specific function and it rarely includes making you look good. However, this is the same for every competitor and what you must understand is that while you may think that other girls look better than you do and you have concerns about how you might look it is not the case in anyone else's eyes. I have been to many athletics meets and seen a lot of shapes and sizes and have never once heard a comment about how someone looks in terms of whether they look good aesthetically or not. **No-one cares**. All that people are interested is in whether someone is short or tall, muscular or lean and all this is in terms of weighing up competitors for their event. You might be short for a high jumper or lean for a shot putter but even that is only an appraisal against perceived performance and is immediately updated on watching actual performance. I have never heard of anyone who is not good looking enough to be a hurdler or who does not wear their crop top well enough to throw a javelin correctly. It is unimportant. The only figures that matter are the ones that are recorded for sporting purposes, like points scored or distance thrown.

In this book, no particular emphasis has been placed on any of the approaches, but if you are female and you suffer from a lack of self-esteem or self confidence and your competitiveness is less than your male counterparts, this will soon become a constraint on your performance and you must recognise it as such and follow the steps in the overcoming weaknesses chapter to overcome it. Do not compare yourself to other girls as this is the norm. Compare yourself to elite performers like Jessica Ennis and Ellie Simmonds and make improvements based on those comparisons.

Appendix 3 – For the parents

Being a parent of an elite, aspiring athlete is not easy. Whether you are Peter Coe (Seb), Judy Murray (Andy), Debbie Daley (Tom) or Bert le Clos (Chad), it is a difficult role to play. You have to be supportive, without interfering, helping to push them along, without living their dreams for them. You endure all the pain but hide it from them.

But on the other hand, in my experience, and if you watch the video of Bert le Clos from the BBC interview, our ecstasy is greater than even the athletes themselves. Having read the Unknown Olympian and talked to athletes, the overwhelming feeling of the athlete on their achievements is one of relief. The elation is more slow-burning. The initial feeling is that it is over (for now), that the training worked and it was all worthwhile. This is similar to the build up where, although athletes get nervous, it is nothing compared to us parents.

So, why the difference? The primary reason is that for the athlete it is a process that they are engaged in over a long period, it is progressive and culminates in the performance. They know exactly how hard they have worked and their expectations (normally) are based on that knowledge. Therefore, the excitement level is tempered by preparation.

For us parents, it is very different. We haven't done all the training and although we are involved in some way, the simple fact is it is not us. What this means is that for us, the feelings are extremely intense, being as they are, compressed into a much shorter timescale. Watching, as a coach or a parent, we can only stand by, impotent while our charges get on with what they have trained for. When they get to the end of the game or race, they are physically spent. We, on the other hand, are emotionally spent instead.

So what does it take to support your child through to an elite level? For a start, you are on the right track, as you have shown immense good judgement in buying this book! Knowledge is power and you are researching, which is very positive.

The most important thing you can do as a parent, and probably the most difficult, is to let them do their own thing (within reason). You can only encourage them; you cannot direct them when it comes to their sport. They might be good at one sport but want to play another. Even if you disagree, you cannot interfere too much. Trust me when I tell you, the risk outweighs the possible gain.

Over and over I have seen kids pushed by their parents when they have wanted to change direction and have eventually just stopped playing. If you push too hard you will get a backlash eventually and it will possibly be extreme. Read the chapter on motivation again. You need to understand that the overall motivator has to be intrinsic. They have to want it for themselves. If you feel you want it more than them, you need to back off a little. Sometimes they cannot see what you see and you have to be patient. Remember being the best at a young age can be a major disadvantage as much as an advantage. Play the longer game. It is more important that they love the sport, it will sustain them longer.

As a couple of personal examples, my son was a short sprinter when he was younger but I could see that with his height and build he would be a better long sprinter. I suggested it to him but he wasn't interested. I had to wait. It took a whole year before he tried it and then he stunned us all, himself included, with his performance, winning a national medal 8 weeks after his first 400m race. But what I learned from that is not that I was right, but actually that it is more likely that he was. Firstly, because it wasn't until he was ready to try it that it would have worked anyway, and secondly, if he had started earlier, would he have had the same development path? Possibly not. Of course, I tell him that I was right all along and he is just slower to realise than I am, even though I do not believe that.

The other example was that even after he was performing at national level, he was also still playing football. Having been very badly injured myself at 16 playing football I feared injury for him. My wife and I discussed this at length and it was a really difficult thing for me not to push him into making a decision. I wanted him to give up but I couldn't tell him. For a time he was approached by scouts of professional clubs which made my nervousness worse, but I was worried that either he would go the wrong way (football is not a sport I wanted him to pursue) or he would resent being pushed into a decision. I managed to hold my nerve (just) and two relatively minor injuries early in one football season badly affected his winter sprint training. He realised he couldn't continue so he gave up. Once the decision was made, it was final for him and he stopped after the next game, much to my relief.

In both cases, holding my counsel was difficult but absolutely the right thing to do (although without my wife's guidance I would have struggled much more in the second example). It is far better for the kids to make their own decisions. It is not the same as schoolwork or health or their lifestyle, which are what we parents are here for – to provide robust guidance and direction where necessary. This is about something they have to commit to themselves and want for themselves.

As parents, our job is to supply money. We are their sponsors and financial support in their early years (for which we will get little thanks!), although I did recently see an athlete at an area championships warming up with a tee-shirt that had "Main Sponsors – Mum and Dad" on it which amused me. Sport costs. Even the sports that do not seem to cost much still cost; clothing, equipment, subscriptions, entry fees. The higher the level, the greater the cost, with further to travel, more expensive equipment and higher subs. All the caveats on sacrifice for the athletes in Chapter 6 – Sacrifice apply to parents as well. You sacrifice your time, your money, and sometimes your own dreams and aspirations to give your kids the support they need.

Giving them support though is more than just about money and transport. You have to encourage them to have a learning mentality. Encourage their effort, not their achievements. Encourage them to strive for better, to try and try, to fall over like the ice skater, but, in doing so, to improve. Pick them up each time they fall, dust them off and start them off again, encouraging the attempt, not the outcome. Help them develop their growth mentality in all things and they will improve not just in their sport but in all things. When kids think they are talented, they tend not to work as hard. They feel that their "natural talent" will get them through. If talent is natural, when it runs out, there is nothing you can do. Whereas if talent is earned through work and practice then hitting an obstacle or a problem that is difficult or never seen before, is just something that can be overcome through more work or practice. This is the ethos that parents need to encourage in their children.

Understand the pitfalls of how praise is given. If all the praise and accolades comes to you for being the best or for winning, then why risk not winning? Why would you put yourself in a position to be anything other than the best? To get kids to keep pushing themselves to the next level is more than just encouraging them to do so, it cuts to the heart of our value system. We need to praise and reward the effort and the improvement, not the result. The results will come in time but they are secondary to improvement.

To help them to the next level, as parents, we need to facilitate their ideas. If they are ready to move on or to improve, we can give them guidance; help them to find what they need. Talk to the coaches in a way only an adult can, especially if your child is a pre-teen or a young teenager.

Lastly, sport is made up of highs and lows. Some of the highs are extremely high and conversely the lows can be extremely low.

"If you can meet with triumph and disaster, and treat those two imposters just the same" – Rudyard Kipling (1885-1936) English author and poet.

Teenage years are full of extremes of emotion, so sporting triumphs or disasters can be magnified. As parents we need to let our teenagers exercise their chimp. Get the whole thing out of their system and let the chimp loose until it is ready to go back to sleep. Encourage this in a "safe place" whether that is the car on the way home or somewhere equally comfortable. You can be their safe person. Do not try to debate or discuss until the chimp has exhausted itself and the human has taken over (if at this point this is not making any sense, you need to read Chapter 18 – Choking and how to prevent it (The danger of thinking) or better still Steve Peter's book "Chimp Paradox"). By all means prompt and ask open questions and let the chimp jabber on no matter how illogical. Once it has had a good run around unfettered and it has tired itself out, you can then discuss the performance with the human portion of your child logically. It is a waypoint and good or bad, it just is what it is and is no more than that.

Whatever we do and do not do as parents has such an immense influence on our kids lives and their chances of success that we need to take care with the 'how'. But at the end of the day, take delight in the progress your kids have made so far. Take a helicopter view of where they are and take a moment to sit back and be proud. All the advice in the above writing is just that, but know this as well: you have got them this far so you must be doing something right!

Acknowledgements

I have been helped over the years by so many people. I have read so many things and learned on so many courses. It would be impossible to acknowledge everyone so at the risk of offending, I would just like to say thank you to those who have helped me directly and indirectly.

In the course of writing this book, I pulled from over a decade of experience and memory. If I have included something you told me, or that you wrote, that I may have scribbled on a piece of paper but forgotten where it came from and so have failed to attribute it properly, then please let me know and I will ensure I correct that in later editions. For my terrible memory, I can only apologise.

"If I have seen further, it is by standing on the shoulders of giants." - Sir Isaac Newton. Physicist and Mathematician (1642 - 1726)

I hope you have enjoyed this book. If you want more information you can find it either on my author website leeness.co.uk or on my sport website newpersonalbest.co.uk

I would be really grateful if you would take a moment to rate this book on whichever site you bought it from. It will make a real difference and any feedback will be taken into account on future editions.

Thank you.

Lee Ness

2014

Printed in Great Britain
by Amazon.co.uk, Ltd.,
Marston Gate.